To everybody who has had to
choose between washing their hair
or making an apple pie.

BIG MAMMA

ITALIAN RECIPES IN 30 MINUTES

➤ SHOWER TIME INCLUDED ➤

WHITE LION
PUBLISHING

BEFORE YOU GET COOKING

WE SHOULD EXPLAIN:

Big Mamma is a gang of around 2,000 merry souls hailing from all four corners of Italy and beyond who enjoy living it up at lunch- and dinner-time in eateries designed to be welcoming and slightly whacky. Fresh produce arrives every day from our long-time suppliers (Stefano Borchini, Lorenzo Bagatto, Salvatore Corso and all the other exceptional artisans who have worked alongside us since the beginning) for use in generous, authentic Italian recipes, passed down in our chefs' families from one generation to the next. United in a single mission: to transport you to Italy and be the best part of your day. A special big-up to Peppe, our ringmaster, to Alberto, the artist of the kitchen, to Monia, a magician with all things sweet, and to Virginia, the high priestess of the cooking stove. Now, on with the show!

4

CONTENTS

'ARE THEY REALLY ARRIVING IN HALF AN HOUR? I HAVEN'T A CLUE WHAT TO COOK! AND – IS THAT WHAT YOU'RE WEARING?'

Does this conversation ring a bell?

It's not always easy to find the time or the motivation (no need to feel guilty) to linger over a hot stove when your mother-in-law has already parked at the end of the street or when the new neighbours are knocking at your door, armed with a bunch of flowers.

But what if we told you that in 20 or 30 minutes flat you could have your guests' mouths watering? *Amici*, we are going to share all our secrets with you: how to save the maximum time possible with 5 kitchen tools that cut corners for when you next cook for your friends – essential Italian equipment that you should always keep at hand; how to make your own limoncello alongside dessert for the coming weekend; how to set a stylish table; and 5 tips for choosing a splendid piece of Parmigiano that's sure to steal the heart of your date.

We asked our chefs to share their favourite Italian recipes, all of which can be made in record time. Alberto extolled the virtues of the veggie carbonara cooked by his *nonna*; Virginia revealed her tricks for conjuring up a pizza from scratch in 28 minutes; Monia showed us how to make her famous chocolatey cheesecake, and Michele gave us tips on how to cook wonderful antipasti and still have time to spruce yourself up before your guests arrive. Put on some background music, uncork a bottle and get out the knives! *Andiamo.*

9 CHEF SECRETS
FOR SAVING TIME

1 You can't become a *Forno* Star without getting the basics right. Before picking up your knife or pizza slicer, first make a shopping list for each stage of your recipe.

2 Tip: always wear an apron over a simple T-shirt. If you splash sauce down your clothes, just rub them with washing-up liquid over the sink – otherwise you'll lose precious time, or any inclination to cook at all.

3 Check your recipe the day before and pre-prepare as many elements as you can. You can make a start on your homemade marinades, stuffings, sauces and doughs before the big day.

4 Gain time whilst seemingly wasting it. Establish your game plan before getting stuck in. And, above all, once you have started cooking, wash up and put away any equipment or ingredients as you go.

5 Need to cook onions? Put a lid on the frying pan to speed up the process. No onions needed? Well, the same is true for many other ingredients like peppers, carrots and even rice.

6 Don't add salt to water until it starts boiling. Salt has a cooling effect on water so, if you add it too soon, you may have to wait even longer for it to boil. And we all know that a watched pot never boils.

7 Cut your vegetables using a mandolin. It's not only quicker but it also means you won't have to spend the night nursing that finger you sliced open with a knife.

8 When using a chopping board, wash after every use. That way you can 'wipe the slate clean', ready for the next step.

9 Cook to music: chop, peel and fry while exulting in the magnificent voice of Pavarotti. *La musica* provides rhythm and makes everything go faster!

HOW TO SELECT YOUR BASIC PRODUCE

1 FIOR DI SALE

Salt, but not just any old salt. You need cooking salt. When you season or dress a dish, use Trapani *fior di sale*.
Tip: don't overload your plate with this diamond of the salt marsh – it's best to go easy with it.

2 CHILLI

Peperoncino, a chilli produced in Calabria, will give plenty of oomph to a spicy oil that can take your pizzas
to another level. In a few pages, you can find out how to make your own.

3 EGGS

Whether you are using them cooked or raw, opt for organic eggs wherever possible.
The difference will be far more noticeable on your plate than in your wallet.
Tip: look for the number written on the shell: 0 = organic, 1 = from free-range chickens.
If it's 2 or over, you're advised to walk on by. If you're in the UK, you may also notice the Lion Mark, which
indicates that the eggs have been produced following strict safety standards. And always remember that even the
best eggs are better for both you and the planet when they are eaten in moderation.

4 OLIVE OIL

A basic olive oil is fine for cooking. However, for dipping bread or finishing off a good tomato and mozzarella
salad, your best bet is extra-virgin olive oil. Keep several different bottles and varieties in your cupboard so you
can create a variety of flavours (and pleasures...).

5 TOMATOES

When it comes to tomatoes, San Marzano is the one!

If your *gastronomia* (local grocer) is out of stock (or they are out of season), you can fall back
on a good homemade sauce. It is vital to make a generous amount in the summer so that you can have
it as a standby throughout the rest of the year.

In short, you can see that our advice is to invest in high-quality ingredients whenever possible: whole black
peppercorns rather than pre-ground; a slightly more expensive tin of tuna for the sake of both your taste buds
and stomach; or an extra-large jar of capers so that you can store them in their brine.
If you use good basic ingredients, your dishes will always be a success.

THE 5 GAME-CHANGING UTENSILS FOR COOKING LIKE A CHEF

1 GRATTUGIA

Or a 'grater' in English. It won't do to live without one, especially given the amount of cheese in Italian cooking. As Shakespeare famously wrote, 'Some are born great, some achieve greatness, and some have a grater thrust upon them.'

2 KITCHEN TONGS

Thin metal ones with round ends, for gripping spaghetti, mixing it thoroughly in a sauce and then serving it straight onto a plate.

3 KNIFE (SHARPENED)

Avoid bargain-basement knives and stay clear
of those with rounded ends. Go for anything
that's really sharp: opt for quality.

4 WOODEN CHOPPING BOARD

In other words, plastic boards are a no-no.
It's better for the planet and the look
of your kitchen. A single board
will last you a lifetime.

5 COPPER FRYING PAN

Perfect for making a risotto, adding the final touch to
pasta dishes and cooking meat. Beware, keep it well away
from the dishwasher!

APERITIVO

VICTOR ED IL CORNETTO

Victor's recipe for ham and Munster cheese croissants

PER 4 AMICI (2 CROISSANTS)

- 2 all-butter croissants
- 100g (3½oz) Munster cheese *(Victor loves Munster, which is why we've chosen it, but there are plenty of other good alternatives. We're still hotly debating which is best.)*
- 200g (7oz) herb-cooked ham
- Cucumber, finely sliced into rounds *(optional)*

1 Cut the croissants in 2 lengthways and divide the Munster equally between each bottom half. Add the ham and close the croissants.

2 If you have a sandwich toaster or panini press gathering dust in your cupboards? Now is the time to use it. Warm your croissants on the toaster grill for 3 minutes. They will come out nicely browned, with the cheese melted. No sandwich toaster? The grill in your oven will work just as well (on a high heat for 5 minutes).

COSTANZA'S TIP

Just before serving, add finely sliced rounds of cucumber to the croissants. A little healthy touch that may (or may not) ease your conscience.

A MINUTE TO SPARE?

Use it to fine-tune your table setting. You can put a *sottopiatto* (service plate) under each of your guests' plates – not for eating off, but as decoration. And if you don't have underplates in your cupboard, you can start drawing up your Christmas gift list, as *piatti*, aka crockery, always comes in handy.

OLIVE YOU

Olives with herbs, fresh chilli and garlic

A recipe from Puglia, for nibbling alongside an aperitif. Treat yourself, as any time is always the right time for a little aperitif. You deserve it.

PER 10 AMICI

- 1kg (2lb 3¼oz) green olives preserved in brine
- 1 garlic clove, finely chopped
- 1 fresh chilli, finely chopped
- 50g (1¾oz) Aleppo chilli
- ½ bunch fresh oregano, finely chopped
- ½ bunch flat-leaf parsley, finely chopped
- 600ml (2½ cups) extra-virgin olive oil
- Salt QB
- Pepper QB
- 1 olive leaf, for garnish (optional)

1   Put the olives in a bowl and add the garlic, fresh chilli (beware, this is hot!), oregano, parsley, olive oil, Aleppo chilli, salt and pepper, and mix thoroughly. Garnish with the olive leaf, if using.

2   *E basta*, it's ready! Transfer to a small ramekin, add the olive leaf, if using, set alongside a glass of spritz, and there you are – in Rome!

A MINUTE TO SPARE?

Watch the video on the Gucci family from Bloomberg: 'The Real Story Behind the *House of Gucci*'.

MEASUREMENTS FOR DUMMIES

Since it is sometimes scary to dive in without having exact quantities, we thought it would be useful to share with you our love of both Q and B.

'QB', what on earth is that? Quanto basta – literally 'as much as required', meaning 'to taste'. True devotees of Italian cooking know that this provides scope to avoid following the rules down to the last detail. You don't have to guess quantities, but you are strongly encouraged to follow your instincts and trust your judgement. It's like riding a scooter in Naples or promising yourself ONE spritz on a terrace and ending up ordering a second – everything is decided on the spur of the moment.

Even so, here are some tips to make cooking your dinner that bit easier:

• Whatever your measuring cup may say, rest assured that, roughly speaking, 1g (gram) = 1ml (millilitre).

• When you come across a bunch or half a bunch of herbs, bear in mind that 1 bunch generally amounts to 100g (3½oz). And, when it comes to the choice of herbs and their quantities, you always have the last word. You decide when enough is enough.

• A teaspoonful of sugar or butter weighs around 5g (under a fifth of an ounce).

• A tablespoonful of oil or vinegar weighs around 15g (just over half an ounce).

• 250ml of milk, cream or water is always the equivalent of 1 glass (unless you only drink pints) or a US cup.

So, now you have the key to make the perfect dish, or almost... Because, really, the most important thing in cooking is to put your heart and soul into it. When you prepare a meal with plenty of love, everything will go smoothly.

QB*

quanto basta = as much as required / to taste

BIG BALLS THEORY

Arancini with Scamorza cheese and Treviso leaves

Fun fact: in Sicily, there is a controversy raging over whether one should say *arancino* (masculine) or *arancina* (feminine)? In Palermo, this delicacy is feminine (*arancina*) and comes in the form of a large ball, but in Catania it is a triangle (in reference to the shape of Mount Etna) called (in the plural) *arancini*. Avoid confusing the two if you want to get out of an Italian deli in one piece.

PER 4 AMICI

- 1 red radicchio (or *Treviso* lettuce, a kind of large pink- and-white chicory popular in northern Italy)
- ½ white onion
- 350g (generous ¾ cup) rice
- 100g (3½ oz) Scamorza (*or a provola affumicata – as it is smoked, the water has already evaporated from the cheese, avoiding any surplus moisture*)
- 20g (¾oz) butter
- 45g (1½oz) grated Parmigiano Reggiano

- 1 glass red or white wine
- 100ml (scant ½ cup) extra-virgin olive oil

For the coating
- 200g (generous 1⅓ cups) plain flour
- 300g (2 cups) breadcrumbs
- 1 glass sparkling water

1
Chop the onion and sauté it in a saucepan in the olive oil. Julienne (slice into thin strips) the red radicchio, add half of it to the saucepan and mix with the onion. Add the rice and toast it over a low heat for 3–4 minutes, stirring continuously with a wooden spoon until it becomes translucent.

2
Deglaze the saucepan with half of the wine, drink the rest (cheers!) and heat the mixture for 3–4 minutes to allow the liquid to evaporate. Add around 500ml (generous 2 cups) hot water and stir. If you think the rice needs a little more cooking, don't worry because it should have a little bite: the rice needs to be crunchy to go onto the next stage. However, if you really think that it is undercooked, add a little more water and cook for another 5–6 minutes. We'll let you be the judge – you're the boss. Add the butter, grated Parmigiano and the rest of the radicchio. Mix, cover the saucepan and leave to rest at room temperature for 4 minutes.

3
Spread the rice out on a baking tray, in a thin layer, to allow it to cool quickly. Make small rice balls (about 50g/1¾oz each), enclosing a small piece of Scamorza inside each one. Once all the balls are ready, mix the flour with the glass of sparkling water in a small bowl until you obtain a smooth batter (neither too liquid nor too creamy).

4
Dip each ball into this mixture and then into the breadcrumbs. Deep-fry the balls in a heavy-based saucepan half-filled with piping hot sunflower oil for 4–5 minutes. Turn the balls regularly to ensure that they are browned on all sides. Remove from the heat and dry the balls on a paper towel in order to remove any excess fat. Eat them with your hands while they are still hot. The arancini should be able to 'make a telephone call', as they say in Italy: you want to be able to see a fat string of cheese, like an old-style telephone cable, when you tear into them.

A MINUTE TO SPARE?

We've snuck in here a recipe for a natural hair mask that you can use after washing your hair. Mix 1 egg yolk, 1 tbsp of olive oil and 1 tbsp of honey. Apply this mixture to your hair and leave in for 30 minutes. Surprising but effective.

PANELLE DI CECI

Chickpea fritters

These little wonders come from Sicily. In Italy, they are eaten in sandwiches along with aïoli. Scrumptious!

PER 4 AMICI

- 500g (3½ cups) chickpea flour
- 1 bunch of parsley, leaves picked and chopped
- 1.3 litres (5½ cups) water

- Sunflower oil QB
- 20g (1 generous tbsp) fine salt

1 Add the chickpea flour to a saucepan of salted water, whisking to avoid any lumps.

2 Simmer over a medium heat, all the while whisking constantly (we're watching you!). When the mixture starts to thicken, leave it to cook for a further 15 minutes, stirring every 2–3 minutes with a wooden spoon.

3 Add the parsley leaves to the saucepan after removing it from the heat. Spread the contents of the saucepan on a baking tray in a layer 3cm (a generous inch) thick and leave to cool at room temperature. When the dough has firmed up sufficiently, cut it into pieces (to whatever size your prefer) and then fry in a deep saucepan half-filled with piping hot sunflower oil.

4 To round off the dish, serve the fritters with a little salsa verde (if you have enough time – see page 286). Put up your feet and enjoy the moment. Just try not to scoff the lot!

A MINUTE TO SPARE?

You can watch the scene in the 1954 comedy *Poverty and Nobility* where the inimitable Italian actor Totò (Antonio de Curtis) slips spaghetti into his pocket to save face as he attempts to win over a beautiful woman and make a good impression on her family.

MOZZARELLINE FRITTE

Breaded mozzarella balls topped with basil pesto

<u>PER 4 AMICI</u>

- 500g (1lb 1½oz) small mozzarella balls
- 2 eggs
- Plain flour QB
- Breadcrumbs QB

- Sunflower oil QB
- *Pesto alla genovese QB (if you have a little extra time, turn to page 284 to find out how to make a really, really good homemade version)*

1
The day before (hopefully you will have opened this book by then): put the mozzarella balls in the fridge, in a colander set over a bowl. Leave them there overnight. The idea is to dehydrate them a little by draining off some of their liquid.

2
On D-day, whisk the eggs, and generously dunk the mozzarella into them, then dip into the flour and, finally, the breadcrumbs. Repeat.

3
Deep-fry the balls in a heavy-based saucepan half-filled with piping hot sunflower oil until browned. Leave to rest for 2–3 minutes before serving. To serve, arrange the *mozzarelline fritte* on a plate in the centre of the table, accompanied by a small bowl of basil pesto.

Attenzione a non scottarvi !

A MINUTE TO SPARE?

Use the time to knock up a non-alcoholic cocktail to get your guests vibing. Mix 60ml (¼ cup) lemon juice and crushed red berries with 5 tsp of cane sugar and 300ml (1¼ cups) of sparkling water, add some ice cubes and then pour the mixture into a glass. Sit back, you're now on holiday.

SPRITZ-TEASE

A little bit of history. In the first half of the 19th century, Venice formed part of the Austrian Empire; Austrian soldiers, officials and tradesmen ruled the roost. These Austrians were not used to the high levels of alcohol in the local wines served in the taverns. Thus began the tradition of asking a waiter 'to water' wine to dilute it. This practice, known as 'spritzen' in German, gave rise to spritz. As there was no Aperol to hand in this period, the resulting cocktail consisted solely of white wine and sparkling water.

So what's the story nowadays? (Venetian) Spritz is an alcoholic cocktail much loved as an aperitif throughout Europe and further afield.

How is it prepared? It consists of a sparkling white wine (normally prosecco) and a bitter liqueur such as Campari (to obtain a dark red colour) or a much sweeter variant, such as Aperol (for a more orangey colour). This enticing mixture is rounded off with a dash of soda water and a slice of fresh orange.

Its less well-known versions include a black, amberish spritz based on Cynar and a white spritz (known as a 'Hugo cocktail' or 'St-Germain spritz') which contains elderflower liqueur.

RECIPE FOR A GOOD SPRITZ
Combine, in the following order:

- A generous helping of ice cubes (enough to fill ¾ of a glass)
- 4.5cl (1½fl oz) Aperol*
- 10cl (3¼fl oz) prosecco
- 5cl (1¾fl oz) sparkling water
- 1 slice of orange or lemon or an olive

* The Aperol can be replaced, in the same proportions, by Campari, St-Germain or Select.

FRISELLE BÜNDCHEN

Crazy slices of toasted sourdough piled with a medley of tomatoes

PER 4 AMICI

- 4 friselle *(available in an Italian gastronomia – deli – but if you can't find them, toasted slices of stale sourdough bread will do)*
- 200g (7oz) Datterini tomatoes
- 1 beef tomato
- 1 bunch Sicilian mountain oregano *(this can be found, but if you can't get hold of it, use standard oregano instead)*
- 1 bunch basil

- 1 tsp white wine vinegar
- 200ml (1 scant cup) extra-virgin olive oil
- Salt QB
- Pepper QB

1
Roughly chop both kinds of tomato any way you wish. This is a very casual recipe. Season with the oregano, basil (saving a fresh leaves for garnish), vinegar, oil, pepper and salt, then mix thoroughly. Dip the friselle into a bowl of cold water for 30 seconds.

2
Drain the friselle and arrange them on a plate, then place the tomatoes on top. Allow the bread to absorb the tomato juices for at least 5 minutes.

3
Dress with the remaining basil leaves (it is impossible to overdo basil). And now, tuck in! Your mission, if you agree to accept it, is to avoid spilling all these lovely little tomatoes on yourself.

A MINUTE TO SPARE?

Tidy your fridge. Are the fruit and vegetables covered by a paper towel or cloth? Have the walls been wiped down with multipurpose spray? Yes? Good, now you're ready to work with us in our kitchen.

CHEESE POPS

Crispy fried Caciocavallo for cheese lovers

PER 4 AMICI

- 500g (1lb 1½oz) Caciocavallo cheese (*if not, Emmental will work fine*)
- 2 eggs
- Plain flour QB
- Breadcrumbs QB
- Sunflower oil QB
- Salt QB
- Pepper QB

1
Cut the cheese into squares of around 4 × 4 cm (1½ × 1½in). Place the eggs in a stainless-steel bowl (or any other to hand), season with salt and pepper, and then beat them with a fork. Dip the pieces of cheese in the flour and then in the egg. Dip them in the egg once again and then, finally, dip them in the breadcrumbs.

2
Fry these lil 'pops' in a heavy-based saucepan half-filled with piping hot sunflower oil for at least 3–4 minutes. Remove and toss quickly on paper towel to dry, and place them as the centrepiece of your table. You are a *pronto* star.

A MiNUTE TO SPARE?

Take a mini-nap before your guests arrive. Best to set the alarm, though.

BRUSCHETTA VITELLO TONNATO

Bruschetta with veal and tuna sauce

PER 4 AMICI

- 2 large slices of sourdough bread
- 240g (8½oz) high-welfare rose veal cushion
- 15g (2 tbsp) anchovy fillets in oil
- 20g (¾oz) capers in coarse salt (these are available in all Italian food shops)
- 250g (9oz) tuna in oil

For the sauce
- 1 egg
- 2 egg yolks
- 1 lemon
- 150ml (¾ cup) sunflower oil, more or less ('a sentimento', as Virginia would say)
- Olive oil QB

1
To cook the vitello: in a frying pan, sear the veal on all sides to brown it thoroughly. Finish cooking it in the oven at 160°C fan/180°C/350°F/GM 4 for 20–25 minutes (it should remain pink in the middle), then remove and leave to cool; collect the juices for use in the salsa tonnata, then slice.

2
For the salsa tonnata: using an electric hand mixer at a medium speed, combine the whole egg and 2 yolks in a bowl. While still mixing, squeeze in a few drops of lemon juice, add the juices from the veal and gradually (and gently) pour in the sunflower oil. The sauce should have the consistency of a mayonnaise.

3
Add the anchovies, tuna and then the capers (rinsed) to the sauce in the bowl. (Our top caper tip is that you need to soak these little gems for a good 5 hours, but as you've only just opened this book and your guests are due to arrive in 24 minutes... Then just give them a good wash.)

4
Mix the sauce again till smooth. To finish, put a drizzle of olive oil into a frying pan and toast the 2 slices of bread until golden brown.

5
Transfer the toasted sourdough to a plate, arrange the slices of veal on top and spoon big dollops of sauce onto the meat (generosity is a virtue!). If you're feeling fancy, a little lemon zest is the ultimate finishing touch. *Sono pronte!*

A MINUTE TO SPARE?

Prepare Bellini cocktails for your guests. These, together with your bruschette, will conjure up the perfect *aperitivo*. Our recipe is: 1 white peach, freshly blended, mixed with 40ml (scant 3 tbsp) crème de pêche liqueur and 400ml (1¾ cup) prosecco, divided between 4 wine glasses.

CROCCHETTE AL TARTUFO

Incredible croquettes with capocollo and black truffle

PER 4 AMICI (12 CROCCHETTE)

- 200g (7oz) capocollo (*which can be replaced by any dryish cooked meat such as Prosciutto di Parma, spianata or salame piccante*)
- 1 large white onion
- 1 medium-size black truffle in season (*around 25g/1oz*)
- 60g (2oz) butter

For the béchamel sauce
- 70g (2½oz) butter
- 70g (½ cup) plain flour

- 450ml (scant 2 cups) whole milk
- Salt QB
- Pepper QB

For the breading
- 1 egg
- 300g (2 cups) breadcrumbs
- Sunflower oil QB

1
  Prepare the béchamel
Melt the 70g (2½oz) of butter in a saucepan. Add the flour then stir with a wooden spoon until you get a smooth paste. Simmer for 1 minute, pour in the cold milk while it is still on the heat and whisk the paste to eliminate any lumps. Cook for 3–4 minutes until thickened. The sauce should be neither too thick nor too runny. Add salt and pepper, then set the béchamel aside at room temperature. We'll use it later.

2
  Thinly slice the onion and soften in a saucepan with 60g (2oz) of butter. Chop the capocollo into small cubes and transfer these (lovingly) to the pan with the butter and onion. Cook for a further 2 minutes. The secret? Do not overcook the cured meat otherwise it'll be too salty. Pour in the bechamel and sprinkle with the grated truffle. Don't worry, you're allowed to use a grater for this – it's not a sin.

3
  Transfer the mixture to the flattest tray you have and allow it to cool. A whole night in a cool place will only improve its consistency (In Italy, we leave it to cool on the balcony), but if you're preparing it to be eaten on the same day, 25 minutes in the freezer will do the trick. After this rest of a few minutes (or a night, depending on your schedule), apply oil to your lovely hands (to stop the mixture sticking to your fingers) and form oblongs of about 5–6cm (2–2½in) long. Dip each in the egg and then in the breadcrumbs, and repeat. Put all the oblongs in the fridge for around 20 minutes before deep-frying them in a heavy saucepan half-filled with piping hot sunflower oil until golden brown. Finally, scatter over a little freshly grated truffle (yes, again! We are obsessed) on top before serving. As much as you want; it's your home after all.

A MINUTE TO SPARE?
Perfect your technique for chopping onions, just don't cry and keep your thumb well out of the way.

ANTiPASTi

YOU'RE THE LIM-ONE

Summer lemon salad

PER 4 AMICI

- 1 lemon per person *(ideally, we advise you to use Procida lemons, which have a distinctive aromatic flesh and a sweet, thick pith)*
- Fresh mint QB
- Chilli QB

- Garlic or spring onions QB
- Extra-virgin olive oil QB
- Salt QB
- Pepper QB

---

1 Peel your lemons without removing the pith (the spongy white layer between the rind and the flesh) and then dice them into cubes (not too small).

2 Soak the lemon pieces in cold water in a salad bowl for 15 minutes. Remove and gently wipe them dry.

3 Season them with the oil, mint, salt, pepper, chilli, and garlic or spring onion.

4 Leave your salad to marinate for 10 minutes, stirring occasionally. And there you have it – the taste of summer!

A MINUTE TO SPARE?

(Re)watch Maradona's goal against England in the quarter-final of the 1986 World Cup – the one that earned him the legendary nickname 'The Hand of God'. A memorable minute of sport.

BURRATINA TURNER

(*So sexy*) breaded burrata

PER 4 AMICI

- 2 burratas (125g/4½oz each – *don't even think of using a 250g/9oz burrata for this recipe*)
- 2 eggs

- Flour QB
- Breadcrumbs QB
- Sunflower oil QB

1
The day before you demonstrate your mastery of Italian cooking (hopefully, you will have opened this book by then), place the 2 burratas in the fridge, uncovered, in a colander set over a bowl. Leave overnight. The idea is to dry them out.

2
On the big day, dip the burratas in the flour until they are well coated, then dip them into the egg. Repeat this, then dip them into the breadcrumbs.

3
Brown the burratas in very hot sunflower oil. Leave to rest for 2–3 minutes before serving.
Open your heart as you open your burratas – and watch how they both start to melt.

A MINUTE TO SPARE?

A riddle. My first part is a scary shout. My second part is a rodent. My third part lies on top of roads. What am I?
Answer: boo-rat-tar. Burratas for ever.

FIORI DI ZUCCA, FARCITI E FRITTI

Fried courgette flowers stuffed with ricotta

PER 4 AMICI (3 COURGETTE FLOWERS PER PERSON)

- 12 courgette flowers
- 350g (12oz) cow's milk ricotta
- 80g (3oz) Parmigiano Reggiano, grated
- 60g (2oz) *provola* (smoked mozzarella)
- Zest of 1 lemon
- 50g (⅓ cup) cornflour

- 300g (generous 2 cups) plain flour
- 1 glass lager
- 1 glass sparkling water
- Salt QB
- Pepper QB
- Sunflower oil QB

1
Open the courgette flowers carefully with the tip of a knife and gently remove their stamen. Cut the provola into squares, put it into a bowl with the ricotta, Parmigiano, lemon zest, and a little salt and pepper. Mix till smooth.

2
Use a piping bag (or a small freezer bag with a corner cut off) to stuff the courgette flowers with the cheese mixture. Fill them up – your generosity will be richly rewarded.

3
Pour half a glass of sparking water and half a glass of lager into a stainless-steel bowl and add all the cornflour.

Whisk. Now add the plain flour, but mix it in with your hands this time to form a batter. In order to achieve a smooth, creamy texture (neither too firm nor too runny), feel free to incorporate more of the remaining water and drink the lager. Or vice versa, as you prefer.

4
As elegantly as you can, dip the courgette flowers into the batter. All that remains now is to fry them in piping-hot sunflower oil for 3 minutes, turning them continuously. Drain, salt, pepper, eat then repeat.

A MINUTE TO SPARE?

Swat up on the following culinary lore so you can impress your dinner guests with your knowledge: *ricotta salata* was born in Sicily. It is made from fresh ricotta (made with the heated whey of ewe's milk), which is salted, pressed and aged for several months. The longer the ageing period, the drier and saltier the end product. This cheese is particularly famous for its contribution to *pasta alla norma* (made with aubergines, tomatoes and ricotta salata).

BRITNEY SPEARAGUS

Asparagus in beurre noisette, with a sprinkling of Parmigiano

PER 4 AMICI

- Around 12 medium asparagus spears
- 100g (3½oz) butter
- 150g (5½oz) Parmigiano Reggiano, grated

---

1 Prep the asparagus by snapping off the woody part, then blanch the spears in boiling water (for about 1½ minutes). Then plunge them immediately into iced water for the same length of time (the best way to preserve a green colour as vivid as a Bottega handbag).

2 Prepare a beurre noisette by heating butter on the stove until golden brown. Arrange the asparagus on a serving dish, drizzle with beurre noisette and cover with ⅔ of the Parmigiano.

3 Put the asparagus under a medium grill for 5 minutes and then sprinkle the remaining Parmigiano on top… Et voilà!

A MINUTE TO SPARE?

Add a poached egg on top of the asparagus so the yolk will run over the dish. Gorgeous.

THE 10 ULTIMATE ITALIAN CHEESES

1 MOZZARELLA This is a bit like potatoes in the UK: I-N-D-I-S-P-E-N-S-A-B-L-E. We opt for mozzarella *'di bufala'* for fresh summer salads, while we prefer mozzarella *'fior di latte'* (in generous quantities) for our *pizze*, as it's less moist.

2 BURRATA The ultimate Eat-Girl for all seasons. This comes from Puglia (hence its southern beauty), where it is zealously applied on top of pasta and focaccias or eaten alone, with a drizzle of extra-virgin olive oil. Always keep it away from the oven, even in winter.

3 RICOTTA Although this is, strictly speaking, a dairy product rather than a cheese, ricotta is the BFF of aubergine and the soulmate of courgette flowers. Ricotta is a breath of fresh air for even the most classic vegetables. It must always be kept in a fridge.

4 MASCARPONE The star of tiramisù, but also a very good substitute for cream in savoury dishes. A jewel of a cream cheese that can enrich your tagliatelle, lasagne and risotto dishes.

5 PARMIGIANO REGGIANO Grate directly over your pasta or add as shavings to your pizzas. Try to buy large blocks whenever possible and invest in a proper Parmigiano grater to grate it as finely as star dust. The golden rule that can never be repeated too often: fish and Parmigiano do not go together. Never, never.

6 PECORINO The saltier cousin of Parmigiano, also unique thanks to its strong taste from sheep's milk. Ever since Roman times, pecorino has been used to accompany chargrilled dishes and the *splendida cacio e pepe*, but it can also be enjoyed on its own as an antipasto. It is crazy good, however, if mixed with Parmigiano in pasta dishes. Thank us later.

7 GORGONZOLA The essential Italian blue cheese, loved for the melody of its name as much as for its flavour. Did you know that it comes from a town of the same name, close to Milan?

8 STRACCIATELLA This is simply the extremely creamy heart of burrata. It's delicious eaten on its own or with *pasta al dente*. So good it'll send shivers up your spine.

9 CACIOCAVALLO This is a vital ingredient in any good *quattro formaggi* pizza. *Bravissimo!*

10 GRANA PADANO Often confused with Parmigiano, this is less fruity and harder. It's perfect for preparing a cheese sauce. Top chefs use high-quality (but reasonably priced) Grana Padano in many wonderful dishes.

PAPPA AL POMODORO

The classic Tuscan dish with tomatoes, bread and Parmigiano Reggiano

PER 4 AMICI

- 400g (14oz) stale bread *(you can ask for this in a bakery or, better still, dry out a sourdough loaf for 24 hours if you have enough time)*
- 800g (1¾lb) vine ripened tomatoes
- 1 white onion
- 100g (3½oz) Parmigiano Reggiano, grated
- Stracciatella QB
- 1 bunch basil
- Extra-virgin olive oil QB

---

1 Finely chop the onion, into about 3mm (⅒ in) pieces, and soften these in olive oil in a saucepan, along with chopped basil stalks (but not the leaves).

2 Slice the tomatoes into quarters, add them to the saucepan with the onions. Simmer for around 5 minutes till softened. Chop the bread into small chunks and add them to the saucepan. Simmer for a further 30 minutes.

3 Remove from the heat and leave to cool for 30 seconds (we know you are in a hurry, but it will be worth the wait). Transfer your pappa al pomodoro to a large bowl, add the basil leaves and Parmigiano and mix the ingredients thoroughly. Add a large glug of olive oil and dollops of fresh stracciatella. A knockout.

A MINUTE TO SPARE?

Remember that stracciatella is the creamy part inside a burrata, not a different type of cheese. It is white and melts in the mouth. Treat yourself to a slice of bread spread with stracciatella before everybody else arrives – you deserve it.

JON BON CHOVY

Anchovy fillets marinated in olive oil, lemon and lime juice

PER 4 AMICI

- 500g (1lb 1½oz) fresh anchovies (*NB: buy them raw – consult your fishmonger*)
- 2 garlic cloves
- 100ml (7 tbsp) lemon juice
- 50ml (3½ tbsp) lime juice
- 30g (½ cup) flat-leaf parsley, finely chopped
- 20ml (4 tsp) white wine vinegar (not red)
- 150ml (⅔ cup) extra-virgin olive oil
- Salt QB
- Pepper QB
- 1 red chilli, chopped finely (*optional*)

1
Tip: the key to this recipe lies in the preparation of the marinade. For this, combine the garlic, parsley, lime juice and 50ml (3½ tbsp) of the olive oil in a blender (no need to faff around with a hand whisk here).

2
Whisk the rest of the olive oil (i.e., 100ml/ 7 tbsp) with the vinegar and the lemon juice to create an emulsion. Combine these 2 mixtures.

3
Remove the heads and spines of the anchovies and then wash them under cold water. Arrange the cleaned anchovies and the marinade in several alternating layers in a baking dish. If you want to add some spice, and a splash of colour, sprinkle some chilli and parsley leaves over your fillets.

4
Leave to rest in the fridge for around 5 hours (or as long as time allows you). After that, '*Carpe diem*' – gather round the table and get stuck in.

A MINUTE TO SPARE?

Take advantage of this downtime to do a bit of sport. No, it's not a joke – you'll sweat but you'll look great. Run to the bakery for various types of bread (walnut, linseed, farmhouse, etc.) then arrange them in a bread basket on the table. Who doesn't enjoy mopping up sauce?

LEEKS GRIGLIATI

Filippo's recipe for charred leeks with stracciatella

PER 4 AMICI

- 4 medium leeks
- 125g (4½oz) stracciatella
- 50g (1¾oz) hazelnuts, toasted
- Zest of 1 lemon
- A selection of fresh herbs (such as chervil, dill, mint and basil)
- Salt QB
- Pepper QB

For the vinaigrette
- 4 tsp extra-virgin olive oil
- 2 tsp white vinegar
- Tarragon, finely chopped QB
- 1 tsp wholegrain mustard
- 1 red onion, finely chopped

1 Put all the ingredients for the vinaigrette in a bowl and beat them vigorously to obtain a stable emulsion.

2 Wash the leeks under cold water, arrange them on a baking tray in the oven and roast them at 190°C fan / 210°C / 410°F / GM 6 for at least 20 minutes (don't worry if they get slightly charred – that's perfectly OK).

3 Remove from the oven and leave to cool for 5 minutes. Once the leeks reach room temperature, remove the outer layer. Slice down the whole length of each leek, open out, put vinaigrette inside then add the stracciatella, the fresh herbs, lemon zest and a few hazelnuts on top. Perfection.

A MINUTE TO SPARE?

It's time to feed your pet. This will stop him/her trying to steal the dessert as soon as you turn your back, and everybody will have a more enjoyable evening. You, him/her and all your guests.

BURRAT-A-DAY
Burrata with button mushrooms

PER 4 AMICI

- ½ kg (1lb 1½oz) button mushrooms
- 4 small *burratine* (125g/4½oz each)
- 60g (2oz) butter
- Sorrel QB, for garnish

- Extra-virgin olive oil QB
- Salt QB
- Pepper QB
- A few buckwheat seeds, for garnish

---

1 Clean the mushrooms with a brush or cloth (never with water, as they will absorb it like a sponge), then sauté them in the butter in a saucepan over a high heat. They must be well browned. Remove from the heat, add salt and pepper. Blend half the contents of the pan with 1 tbsp of water and set aside.

2 Put a few spoonfuls of the mushroom mixture into a bowl, add your plump *burratina*, sliced into 2, then arrange some of the browned mushrooms on top, drizzle with the olive oil and garnish with the sorrel and the buckwheat seeds. Repeat this process with 3 more bowls.

A MINUTE TO SPARE?
Use a mandolin to thinly slice a raw mushroom over the bowls. It looks good, it tastes good – what's not to like?

POMODORI GRATINATI

Roasted tomatoes stuffed with garlic and basil

PER 4 AMICI

- 8 vine ripened tomatoes
- 1 garlic clove
- 70g (2½oz) Parmigiano Reggiano, grated
- 100g (1 cup) breadcrumbs

- 1 bunch basil
- Extra-virgin olive oil QB
- Salt QB
- Pepper QB

---

1 Cut the tomatoes in half horizontally. Use a small spoon to remove their core and pips.

2 With a blender, combine the pulp you've just removed with the garlic. Transfer to a bowl, add the breadcrumbs, basil and Parmigiano and mix thoroughly. Season with salt and pepper.

3 Add this mixture to the centre of each tomato. Drizzle with olive oil then roast these delicious fruits (yes, that's what they are!) on a baking tray in the oven for 15 minutes at around 180°C fan/200°C/400°F/GM 6 and *basta*, they're ready. Now put on some Factor 50 and relax under the Tuscan sun.

A MINUTE TO SPARE?

Have a giggle with Jessie Ware and her mamma Lennie on the podcast *Table Manners*. Our favourite? Supper of tagliata and salsa verde with Stanley Tucci. <3

BURRATA PESTO ALLA GENOVESE

Burrata stuffed with basil pesto

PER 4 AMICI

- 1 large burrata (250g/9oz)
- 100g (scant ½ cup) *pesto alla genovese (turn to page 284 to learn how to prepare a really, really good homemade version)*
- A few basil leaves *(for the visual effect – it can look a bit stark otherwise)*
- Extra-virgin olive oil QB
- Fior di sale QB
- 1 syringe *(if you don't have one handy, you can buy one at a chemist)*

1 Place the burrata on a small round plate and use the syringe to fill it with the pesto. You should need around 50ml (3½ tbsp). A single squirt will be enough (so, easy does it!).

2 Spoon the remaining pesto around the edges of the burrata and scatter the basil on top . Make it rain with olive oil and fior di sale – then tuck in to the nectar of the gods!

A MINUTE TO SPARE?

Read your kid a bedtime story before your guests turn up. This may well be the best part of your evening.

BRUSCHETTA CAPRESE

Bruschetta with mozzarella, basil leaves
and heirloom tomatoes

PER 4 AMICI

- 4 generous slices of sourdough bread
- 2 buffalo mozzarellas (125g/4½oz each)
- 2 large heirloom tomatoes
- Fresh basil leaves QB
- Extra-virgin olive oil QB
- Salt QB
- Pepper QB

1 Heat the oven to 160°C fan/180°C/350°F/GM 4 and toast the slices of bread until they are golden brown.

2 Slice the tomatoes thinly (or thickly – it's your meal) then place them on the warm bread.

3 Tear the mozzarella into pieces and sprinkle generously over the tomatoes.

4 Drizzle on some oil and add a few basil leaves, salt and pepper. Put the slices on a large bread board in the middle of the table, ready to be shared with your loved ones.

A MINUTE TO SPARE?

Fun fact. Although the bidet was invented in France in the 1700s, it really took off in Italy. It's far more than a mini bath for babies, and has become the essential and proper toilet side-kick for any self-respecting Italian. The simple rule: don't go to the loo without visiting the bidet after. That would never do!

5 ITALIAN PRODUCTS YOU SHOULD ALWAYS HAVE IN YOUR CUPBOARD

1 BASIL

This is to Italian cooking what butter is to bread. Always go for fresh basil, on its stalks. Avoid frozen or dried substitutes as much as possible.

2 OLIVE OIL

The magical potion, the ultimate touch that makes Italian recipes so delicious. In the words of our chef Emilia: 'We put it on everything, and we even drink it in the morning.'

3 BLACK PEPPER

This provides the punch to Italian cooking: best bought as whole peppercorns and freshly ground over your steaming-hot dish.

4 PELATI

Your greatest allies in the preparation of the best tomato sauce of your life. Peeled plum tomatoes are sold in delis – if you can, steer clear of any processed alternatives. *'Pelati'* also refers to a group of bald men – which makes sense.

5 PARMIGIANO

The most enticing of all the *formaggi*. We advise you to buy a whole chunk from the fridge section. You will need a proper Parmigiano grater to tame it – it's the weapon of choice for any Italian culinary wizard.

LA DOLCEVICHE

Seabass ceviche and roast pineapple wrapped in Little Gem lettuce leaves

PER 4 AMICI

- 800g (1¾lb) seabass fillet, diced (ask your fishmonger to clean it and prepare it for eating raw)
- ½ red onion, chopped
- 1 lemon
- 1 lime
- 2 heads Little Gem lettuce
- 1 small pineapple (or a big one, if you want some leftovers for the next day's breakfast), diced

- 15g (1 tbsp) butter
- ½ bunch of coriander, finely chopped
- 2 tbsp red wine vinegar
- Extra-virgin olive oil QB
- Fior di sale QB
- Pepper QB

1
30 minutes before the start of the meal (no sooner, no later), pour all the juice of the lemon and juice of half of the lime over the seabass fillet. Grind some pepper over the fish and add some coriander leaves. Leave to rest for around half an hour.

2
Meanwhile, gently heat the red wine vinegar in a saucepan and then pour over the chopped onion.

3
Cut the pineapple into cubes of the same size as the cubes of seabass. Sauté them in a frying pan with the olive oil until they are golden brown.

4
Drain the onion of its vinegar and combine it with both the seabass and the pineapple, mixing thoroughly. Arrange some Little Gem lettuce leaves on a large plate and garnish them with the ceviche. Eat straight away, with your hands: golden finger food.

A MINUTE TO SPARE?

Hit up the internet and look at images of Polignano a Mare, the pearl of Puglia. See you there this summer?

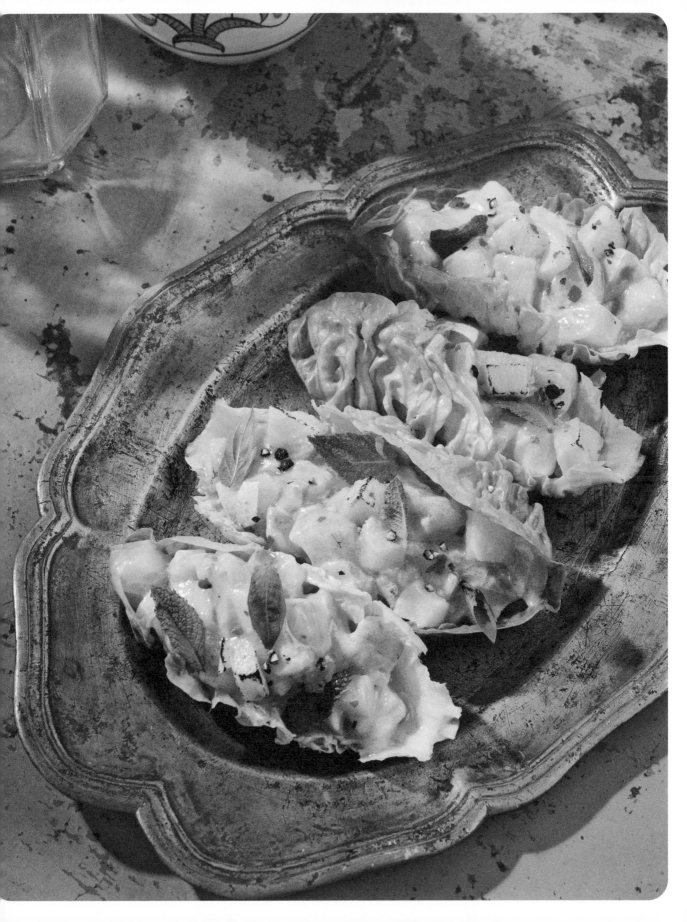

MOZZARELLA TURNOVERS

Puff-pastry turnovers with mozzarella and tomato sauce

<u>PER 4 AMICI</u>

- 2 rolls ready-made puff pastry
- 40ml (2½ tbsp) tomato sauce (*see page 300 for the most delicious tomato sauce recipe in the world*)
- 40g (1½oz) mozzarella
- 15g (½oz) Parmigiano Reggiano

- Basil leaves QB
- Extra-virgin olive oil QB
- Salt QB
- Pepper QB
- 1 tsp milk

1 Spread out the rolls of puff pastry on your worktop. Use a glass to cut out as many small discs as possible. Cover half the discs with a spoonful of tomato sauce, a piece of mozzarella, a few shavings of Parmigiano, some freshly ground pepper, a pinch of salt and a few basil leaves.

2 Finally, cover the discs with their empty counterparts. Use a fork to press down the edges so that the 2 halves are tightly sealed. Use a brush to daub all the turnovers with milk.

3 Place all the turnovers on an oven tray and bake them at 180°C fan/200°C/400°F/GM 6 for 20 minutes. Leave them to rest for 2–3 minutes maximum – and then it's showtime!

Transfer the turnovers to a plate and place this in the middle of the table, so that all your guests can help themselves with their hands.

A MINUTE TO SPARE?

Put on Dalida's version of the song 'Love in Portofino' and twirl around the room to get yourself warmed up for the occasion.

TARTE TATIN DI MANIE

Madeleine's tarte tatin with cherry and datterini tomatoes

PER 4 AMICI

- 400g (14oz) puff pastry
- 400g (14oz) cherry tomatoes
- 100g (3½oz) Datterini tomatoes
- 1 garlic clove, crushed
- 1 bunch dried oregano from the Sicilian mountains
  (otherwise, fresh oregano from your deli – but you can always dream)

- 60g (2oz) feta *(optional)*
- 1 tbsp balsamic vinegar
- Extra-virgin olive oil QB
- Salt QB
- Pepper QB
- 1 tsp white or brown sugar

1
First, make sure you have a frying pan that can go on the stove and also fit in the oven. If you don't have anything suitable, then ask your neighbour – the one who always says hello and seems friendly.

2
Using this frying pan, pour in a little olive oil and then add the oregano, garlic, cherry and Datterini tomatoes cut in half, a pinch of salt and the sugar. Allow this mixture to caramelize over a low heat. A little tip: place the tomatoes in the frying pan on their 'butts' – their round bases – and not on their cut sides. However, if you've already placed them with their flat sides facing down, don't try to turn them over – sometimes you just have to see your decisions through.

3
When the mixture starts to take on a pretty caramel colour, deglaze it with the balsamic vinegar. Then place the puff pastry straight onto the frying pan in order to cover the tomatoes; make sure that all the contents of the pan are completely hidden by the pastry. If not, your tarte Tatin could cause a scene by falling apart.

4
Then make 3 or 4 tiny holes (no more) in the pastry with a fork to stop it swelling too much. Put the frying pan, complete with the tarte Tatin, in the oven for 30 minutes, in conventional mode. If your oven does not have this option, 140°C fan/160°C/325°F/GM 3 in a convection oven for 25 minutes will work just as well.

5
Remove the frying pan from the oven and leave the tart to rest for 2–3 minutes. Turn out the still-warm tarte Tartin from the pan, by covering the pan with a plate and then turning it upside down. To take it to the next level, drizzle on a little olive oil, add a pinch of salt, a few oregano leaves and, if you fancy, a sprinkling of feta – and *buon appetito*!

A MINUTE TO SPARE?

It's time to call that friend who's always late and ask them to atone by stopping off at a wine store. Tell them to get a tasty digestif that will spend the meal in the freezer and then make a surprise entrance along with the dessert. You can suggest any one of the following: mandarinetto, cannellino, Italicus Rosolio di Bergamotto, limoncello, grappa, mirto, nocino, rabarbaro or Frangelico (a hazelnut delicacy that always goes down well).

PIADINA ROMAGNOLA

Romagna-style flatbread wraps stuffed with mozzarella and prosciutto crudo

PER 4 AMICI

- 4 piadine (similar to Mexican tortillas but typically Italian – you can make them yourself easily enough, except that you probably won't have time for a shower)
- 2 buffalo mozzarellas (125g/4½oz each)

- 200g (7oz) Prosciutto di Parma
- 100g (3½oz) rocket
- Tomatoes, if you like (although our chef Giuseppe does not approve, so we've left them out)

1 Put a *piadina* in a hot frying pan for around 2 minutes. Add some pieces of mozzarella and allow them to melt.

2 Remove the flatbread from the frying pan, add the ham and the rocket (and the tomatoes, if using), and then fold over the *piadina* to enclose them inside it. Repeat this for each *piadina* – *presto*, before the first one gets a chance to cool. Then tuck in.

A MINUTE TO SPARE?

Prepare negroni for your guests. Mix the following in a cocktail shaker: 3cl (2 tbsp) each of gin, Campari and vermouth, a few cardamom seeds crushed in a mortar and some ice cubes; pour into a glass then repeat the operation for each guest who's partial to this Milanese aperitif. If you're really ahead of yourself, you can also cook an artichoke in salted boiling water, cut it into large pieces then infuse it with vermouth in a carafe for several hours. Then strain the vermouth and add it to the cocktail.

CAVOLO RIPIENO

Cabbage leaves stuffed with mozzarella, olives, capers and Parmigiano

PER 4 AMICI

- 1 Savoy cabbage
- 300g (11oz) stale bread (*2 options: ask a bakery for some or leave some sourdough bread to dry out for 2–3 days*)
- 70g (generous ⅓ cup) Taggiasche olives, chopped
- 30g (4 tbsp) capers preserved in salt, chopped
- 200g (7oz) mozzarella, torn into small pieces
- 70g (2½oz) Parmigiano Reggiano, grated

- 1 egg
- 20g (¾oz) butter
- 200ml (1 cup) whole milk
- ½ bunch parsley, finely chopped
- Salt QB
- Pepper QB

1
Remove whole leaves from the Savoy cabbage (without damaging them, as if you were detaching cheques from a cheque book). Blanch the leaves in salted boiling water for 1½ minutes, then transfer them immediately to a bowl of iced water to preserve their green colour. Drain and put aside.

2
Cut the stale bread into large pieces and leave them to soak in a bowl of milk for around 4–5 minutes, in order to rehydrate them.

3
Chop the capers and olives then add them to the bowl of milk along with the egg, the mozzarella, some of the Parmigiano, the parsley and the salt and pepper. Beat this mixture to obtain a paste.

4
A word of caution as now we're coming to the folding part – so you'll need to pay attention! Put a mound of the bread mixture (around 7cm/2¾in long and 3cm/1¼in wide) on the lower part of a cabbage leaf (if necessary, you can use a piping bag or a small freezer bag with one corner cut off). Fold both sides of the cabbage leaf inward then roll up to cover the mixture evenly and create a wrap. Repeat this until all the filling and cabbage leaves have been used up.

5
Arrange the wraps in a baking tray, spread butter on top, sprinkle on the remaining Parmigiano and bake them in a convection oven at 170°C fan/190°C/375°F/GM 5 for 15 minutes. Serve the cabbage wraps on a large plate in the centre of the table and get stuck in.

A MINUTE TO SPARE?

Fun fact: Alessio's mother specially cuts up pieces of fresh bread every week and leaves them out to go stale. She then stores them in a glass jar, before using them to make the best croutons on earth. You can start following her example and build up a stock for future occasions.

CARPACCIO DIEM

Sea bass carpaccio with Taggiasche olives, capers and Datterini tomatoes

PER 4 AMICI

- 800g sea bass fillet (*inform your fishmonger that it must be suitable for eating raw*)
- 125g (4½oz) Datterini tomatoes
- 50g (½ cup) Taggiasche olives
- 30g (4 tbsp) capers preserved in salt
- 1 pinch sugar

- Basil QB
- Fior di sale
- Extra-virgin olive oil QB
- Salt QB
- Pepper QB

1
Slice the sea bass fillet into pieces and arrange on sheets of greaseproof paper. Flatten the fish pieces as much as possible with a meat tenderizer.

2
Take half the Datterini tomatoes, slice them in half and season with oil, salt, pepper and sugar. Transfer the tomatoes to an oven heated to 170°C fan/190°C/375°F/GM 5 for a maximum of 4–5 minutes. You want these to burn slightly - so they have a nice blackened finish.

3
Roughly slice the remaining, uncooked tomatoes. Season them with basil, fior di sale, pepper, oil – and plenty of love. Leave the caramelized tomatoes to cool then combine them with their raw counterparts.

4
Delicately spread the fish carpaccio onto a beautiful plate, sprinkle over fior di sale, oil, pepper, olives, capers, the tomato mixture and some small basil leaves. The result should be worthy of Picasso – we're counting on you. After that, all that remains is to call your friends to the table and enjoy.

A MINUTE TO SPARE?

If you're not planning to take a shower before the grand arrival of your guests, you can nevertheless have a peek at your belly button, as sometimes it can accumulate a good deal of fluff from your sweaters. Hairy-chested people seem the most susceptible, ask Filippo…

PRIMI

SPAGHETTI AL LIMONE

Spaghetti with Procida lemon, the traditional recipe

PER 4 AMICI

- 500g (1lb 1½oz) spaghetti
- 2 Procida lemons (*if these are unavailable, you can use other varieties, provided they're unwaxed*)
- 1 garlic clove
- Chilli flakes QB
- Mint, finely chopped QB

- Basil (*optional*)
- Extra-virgin olive oil QB
- Salt QB
- Pepper QB

1
Finely dice 1 of the lemons and transfer to a pestle and mortar. Bash the lemon along with the garlic, chilli flakes, olive oil, salt and pepper. When the ingredients are thoroughly mashed together, transfer the mixture to a frying pan and sauté gently in olive oil with the juice of the other lemon.

2
Add the spaghetti to a saucepan of salted boiling water, but remove and drain the pasta a few minutes before it is completely cooked (reserve some of the cooking water – it will come in handy in the next step).

3
Put the spaghetti into the lemon mixture in the frying pan, pour in some of the reserved cooking water and stir ('*mantecare*', as they say in Italian). A few seconds before turning off the heat, sprinkle on the mint and basil leaves (if using).

4
Serve the spaghetti in pasta bowls, adding a drizzle of olive oil to each – and enjoy! It tastes like a summer holiday, right?

A MINUTE TO SPARE?

Here are the first names of some of our Italian chefs so you can choose 1 or 2 of them to bestow on your future children. We don't want to pressure you, but if you do pick one, your child will be the coolest kid on earth: Virginia, Monia, Stefania, Brenda, Lucia, Andrea, Luca, Alberto, Leonardo, Mattia.

BIG VEGGIE CARBONARA

Veggie spaghetti alla carbonara with fried courgettes, for friends of the earth

PER 4 AMICI

- 500g (1lb 1½oz) spaghetti
- 4 beautiful courgettes
- 6 egg yolks
- 250g (9oz) pecorino, grated (*you'll maybe have some left over for the next day*)

- Sunflower oil QB
- Pepper, in abundance (carbonara *comes from carbone, or 'coal', so don't skimp*)

1
Use a mandolin to cut the courgettes into 3mm (¹⁄₁₀ in) thick round slices. Sauté them in piping-hot sunflower oil in a frying pan until they start to turn golden brown, then set aside.

2
Place the spaghetti into a saucepan of slightly salted boiling water for as long as required. (Be aware that you have to taste pasta to know whether or not it's cooked.) Stir the spaghetti occasionally (we're watching you!). While the spaghetti is cooking, quickly put the egg yolks, pecorino and pepper into a bowl large enough to hold the entire dish. Once the spaghetti is cooked to your satisfaction, remove it from the heat and drain.

3
Transfer the cooked spaghetti straight to the bowl and mix thoroughly. Grind some more pepper on top, add the fried courgettes and place the bowl in the centre of the table.

4
Stir and serve. Don't dawdle – this dish needs to be eaten hot. And, above all, leave any cream out of sight, well away from this recipe and your worktop, just in case an Italian happens to pass by.

A MINUTE TO SPARE?

Arrange some dried flowers and nuts (almonds, walnuts, etc.) in a strip along the entire length of the table. It will look pretty, and the nuts can even be nibbled away at the end of the meal. If you don't have any flowers or nuts to hand, then opt for some crisps. After all, is there any real difference between a rose petal and a fried potato petal? It's the thought that counts.

SPAGHETTI ALL' ARRABBIATA

Spaghetti with tomato sauce, garlic and fresh chilli: for thrill-seekers.

PER 4 AMICI

- 500g (1lb 1½oz) spaghetti (*thick dried spaghetti, as these will suck up the sauce*)
- 1 tin of tomatoes (*or 400ml/1⅔ cups of the superb tomato sauce for which there's a recipe on page 300*)
- 1 garlic clove, crushed

- 2 fresh chillies, finely chopped
- Black olives QB (*optional*)
- Capers QB (*optional*)
- Extra-virgin olive oil QB
- Salt QB

1
Drizzle some olive oil into a saucepan and sauté the finely chopped chillies, tomatoes (or tomato sauce) and garlic clove and simmer for 20 minutes.

2
Meanwhile, cook the spaghetti in a saucepan of boiling water until perfectly *al dente*. Drain the spaghetti and add to the pan with the other ingredients. If a little cooking water goes in as well, that's all to the good. The sauce, the sauce, my kingdom for a sauce!

3
An optional addition that looks great and tastes great: add a few black olives and capers to the sauce – this will give you the levelled up Pokémon version, the *puttanesca*!

Gather your lovers, best friends, foes and family round the table – it's time to put your differences aside, and get stuck in.

A MINUTE TO SPARE?

Put a slice of bread on side plates and a small bowl of extra-virgin olive oil in the middle of the table. It'll make the 'foodies' happy, and will also cool down the flames for any guest who finds the chilli too hot to handle.

THE 8 ITALIAN FILMS YOU NEED TO SEE AT LEAST ONCE IN YOUR LIFE

1   LA GRANDE BELLEZZA 142 minutes of partying. A sublime film about Jep Gambardella, a cynical socialite, who, after spending most of his life surrounded by glitz and glamour, begins to question his existence and his values. The introspective meditations of a 65-year-old man, as he wanders through the heart of Rome, are put under the microscope of the (very) brilliant director Paolo Sorrentino. A special mention for the scene in which Gambardella discovers the photography exhibition under the loggia of the Villa Giulia.

2   CINEMA PARADISO A veritable hymn to life telling the story of a film-crazy young boy who is taken under the wing of a projectionist (played by Philippe Noiret) – and who grows up to be the film's prodigious director, Giuseppe Tornatore. A meta-story that reveals the birth of the director's passion for cinema. We particularly like the scene of the improvised screening in the village square.

3   LA VITA È BELLA Probably the finest depiction ever of the love between a man, his wife and their son. We do not have the words to describe this masterpiece, other than to say *'buongiorno principessa'*. Be sure to have a packet of tissues handy when you watch it. An ode to life that is still unsurpassed.

4   È STATA LA MANO DI DIO A delicate, personal film from Sorrentino showing the adolescence of Fabietto and the arrival of the great Maradona in Napoli – an event that would bring hope and pride to an entire population, starting with Fabietto himself. A special mention for the last scene, in which *'non ti disunire Fabio'* can be heard in the most beautiful spot in the entire city of Naples.

5   IL POSTINO A celebration of poetry in which Pablo Neruda transmits his passion for literature to the local postman on Procida, the island off Naples where he was living in exile. It is impossible to forget the most famous bicycle in history (still on display in Procida). Massimo Troisi, who played the postman, unfortunately didn't live long enough to enjoy the huge success of the film, which he completed against all the odds while suffering from heart disease.

6   IL CAIMANO A political satire loaded with metaphors that explores the story of Silvio Berlusconi without ever mentioning him by name. A biting portrait of Italian society by the master director Nanni Moretti, with the actor Silvio Orlando as his avatar.

7   LA DOLCE VITA If there is one film that you really must see in your lifetime, this is probably it. Fellini's masterpiece made the Trevi Fountain the most famous in the world. We're obviously referring to the magical scene with Anita Ekberg and Marcello Mastroianni.

8   AMICI MIEI The annual get-together of a bunch of friends, directed by Mario Monicelli, who brings to life the memorable pranks of these 5 men. Special mentions for the *supercazzola* scene with the policeman and the train scene, where the farewells take an unexpected turn. You are advised to brush up your Italian in order to grasp all the film's subtilties and appreciate just how funny it is.

RIGATONI ALLA VODKA ANNI 80

Rigatoni with tomato and vodka sauce: enjoy in moderation

PER 4 AMICI

- 500g (1lb 1½oz) rigatoni
- 400ml (1¾ cups) tomato sauce *(see page 300 for the best tomato sauce recipe in the world)*
- 200ml (generous ¾ cup) single cream
- 20g (¾oz) butter
- 1 shallot *(not too small)*, chopped
- ½ glass vodka
- ½ bunch chives, chopped *(optional)*
- Salt QB
- Pepper QB

1
Cook the rigatoni in a saucepan of salted boiling water until *al dente*. In another saucepan, brown the shallot in the melted butter.

2
Deglaze the shallot pan with the vodka. Whilst you wait, pour yourself a shot. *Cin cin!* Add the tomato sauce and cream, and simmer over a low heat for 5 minutes.

3
Roughly drain the pasta (putting aside a little of the cooking water) and add it to the saucepan with the sauce. If the sauce is too thick, you can add half a ladleful of the cooking water. Grind over a little pepper and, if you're fond of greenery, sprinkle over some chives, too – this is truly a disco recipe!

A MINUTE TO SPARE?

Look up the Instagram account @pastagrannies. It's exactly what it says on the tin: pasta plus grandmothers.

10 RULES FOR MAKING AN AUTHENTICALLY ITALIAN CARBONARA

1 Opt for guanciale. The guanciale needs to be cut into strips then put into a frying pan to brown and crisp (no need to add any oil or other fat). Remember that the word *guanciale* comes from the Italian *guancia*, which means 'cheek'. Yes, this tasty morsel we love to use in our cooking is in fact pig's cheek or jowl (*maiale* in Italian) that has been salted then dried. This makes it very different from both pork loin and pancetta (taken from the fatty part of the belly).

2 Eggs. Organic and local whenever possible. The yolks play the starring role here, resulting in a creamier, lighter texture. Our chef Giacomo recommends using 1 whole egg and 3 yolks in a dish for 4 people.

3 Carbonara means pecorino! Forget about Parmigiano Reggiano or any other cheese that doesn't answer to the name Pecorino Romano. If you really want excellence, try to buy DOP.

4 Black pepper, the trump card. There's no Bonnie without Clyde, and no carbonara without black pepper.

5 Watch out for scrambling! To prevent the eggs overcooking, you have to whip them thoroughly with the pecorino in a bowl, away from the stove. When the pasta is al dente, drain it and mix everything together – well away from the hob.

6 No cream, ever, ever! It is the eggs and the pecorino that make this dish creamy. If you want an even more luscious dish, add 1 tbsp of the cooking water from the pasta.

7 Spaghetti, tonnarelli, rigatoni: tradition has it that long pasta is best suited to a carbonara.

8 No onions. Even though we like this addition, carbonara purists insist that this is no place for onions.

9 Chilli does not appear on the guest list. Black pepper should be the only standout taste. There is no room for interlopers.

10 *Pasta al dente: pasta scotta* (overcooked pasta) is always unforgivable, but it's doubly so in a carbonara.

RISOTTO AL FUNGHI

The mushroom risotto that will win everyone over

PER 4 AMICI

- 420g (2 cups) Carnaroli, Vialone Nano, Roma or Baldo rice (*avoid precooked rice*)
- 140g (5oz) butter
- 120g (4oz) Parmigiano Reggiano, grated
- 1 shallot, chopped
- 500g (1lb 1½oz) button mushrooms
- 50ml (3½ tbsp) white wine
- 800ml (3½ cups) vegetable stock
- 1 bunch thyme
- Salt QB
- Pepper QB

1 Quarter the mushrooms and sauté them in a frying pan with 20g (¾oz) of butter and the thyme until golden brown. Set aside, reserving a small handful as your garnish.

2 Soften the shallot in a deep saucepan or casserole dish with 20g (¾oz) of butter then add the rice. Toast the rice for 2–3 minutes, stirring continuously (stay focused, nobody likes burned rice).

3 Deglaze the pan with the white wine. Once the wine has evaporated, add half the sautéed mushrooms and a pinch of salt. Pour in 200ml (¾ cup) of vegetable stock and stir. Repeat this at least 3 times, whenever the liquid evaporates. The rice should cook in the saucepan for around 15–17 minutes, without ever burning or drying. Continue stirring throughout, otherwise you'll end up wasting good wine without any risotto. Take the remaining sautéed mushrooms, blend them with a little stock (or, in its absence, hot water) to obtain a smooth purée.

4 Taste the rice and, if it's ready, switch off the heat, add the Parmigiano, the mushroom purée and the remaining butter. Cover the risotto with a tea towel for 1½ minutes.

5 The big moment has come: remove the tea towel and stir the rice. Plate up the risotto, adding a quartered mushroom to each serving as a garnish. If you truly love your guests, or just want to show off, now's the time to complete the garnish with some shaved truffle. After all, they deserve it!

A MINUTE TO SPARE?

Go and brush your teeth or change your shirt. Anything to stop fretting about how the risotto will turn out.

GIRELLE WOODS

Girelle stuffed with slow-cooked rabbitt

PER 4 AMICI

- 500g (1lb 1½oz) fresh egg pasta *(see page 290 to find out how to make this at home)*
- 300g *cooked coniglio alla ligure (see page 140)*
- 150g (½ cup) ricotta *(see page 120… no, only joking!)*
- 100g (3½oz) Parmigiano Reggiano, grated
- 50g (1¾oz) butter
- 1 red onion

- 20g (scant 2 tbsp) Taggiasche olives
- 20g (2½ tbsp) pine nuts, toasted
- Zest of 1 lemon
- 1 bunch marjoram
- 1 bunch oregano
- Salt QB
- Pepper QB

---

1 Prepare the stuffing the day before

Shred the cooked rabbit meat and mix it with the ricotta, the grated Parmigiano and half the lemon zest. Chop the red onion and gently brown it in a saucepan in 10g (2 tsp) of butter. Finely chop half the marjoram and half the oregano. Add the onion and the herbs to the rest of the stuffing, along with salt and pepper. Combine all the ingredients thoroughly, then set aside.

2 Make the girelle

Roll out the pasta dough so that it is 2mm (¹/₁₀in) thick. Cut into 4 equal strips at least 50cm (20in) long and 13cm (5½in) wide. Put the stuffing into a piping bag (or a small freezer bag with a corner cut off) and squeeze out a sausage 45cm long (18in) and 3cm (1in) wide onto one of the strips. Take care to leave the last 2–3cm (¾–1in) of all the edges of the pasta free from stuffing so that you can do the following manoeuvres successfully. Join the sides of the pasta strip together to enclose the stuffing. Cut off any excess pasta from the ends (remembering to leave a space of around 2cm (¾in) between the stuffing and the edge of the pasta) and from the sides, and then seal the 2 ends tightly. (Most importantly, keep any leftover pasta to make a quick dish of wonderful tagliatelle for lunch the following day.) Wind one girella around itself on the worktop, forming a snail shape. Repeat this with all the strips.

3 When your guests are at their places around the table, immerse the 4 girelle in hot, bubbling salted water for 2 minutes. Take them out of the water, drain and transfer them straight to your plates. Set aside. You're nearly there – don't drop the pace now! Over a high heat, melt the remaining butter in a saucepan and sauté the olives, pine nuts and oregano, along with a few sprigs of marjoram, for 2 minutes. When this mixture starts to turn golden brown, pour some of it over each *girella* in turn. *Si mangia!* After receiving applause from all your guests, obviously.

A minute to spare?

You can always uncork a bottle of good red wine to let it breathe for a while. Pour yourself a small glass, as you thoroughly deserve it – *Cin-cin!*

RISOTTO ALLA MONZESE

Risotto with sausage and red wine

PER 4 AMICI

- 420g (2 cups) carnaroli, Vialone Nano, Roma or Baldo rice *(avoid precooked rice)*
- 140g (5oz) butter
- 120g (4oz) Parmigiano Reggiano, grated
- 1 shallot, chopped
- 250g (9oz) sausage

- 50ml (3½ tbsp) red wine
- 800ml (3½ cups) vegetable stock
- Salt QB
- Pepper QB

1
Squeeze out the sausage meat and sauté until it is golden brown in a deep saucepan or casserole dish. Add the shallot and soften.

2
In the same saucepan, toast the rice for 2–3 minutes, stirring continuously (don't get distracted, otherwise the rice will burn). Deglaze with the red wine. Once the wine has evaporated, add a pinch of salt and a little pepper.

3
Pour in 200ml (¾ cup) of vegetable stock and stir. As soon as the water has evaporated, pour in another batch. Repeat this at least 2 more times. The rice should take 15–17 minutes to cook. Keep stirring it all the time. It mustn't burn or dry up. Stay on the alert for the sake of your risotto – it's well worth the effort.

4
Taste the rice. Once it's ready, remove it from the heat, add the butter and sprinkle on the Parmigiano. Cover the risotto with a tea towel. After 1½ minutes, stir the rice vigorously. Serve the risotto on individual plates, *e basta*.

A MINUTE TO SPARE?

The reason why Italians are so expressive with their hands can be traced back to the country's repeated historical invasions. As the changes in language were difficult to assimilate to, people grew used to 'speaking' with their hands to make themselves understood. Even today, there are still over 35 different dialects spoken across The Boot. So, here's a trick, the best way to make an Italian shut up is by tying their hands!

GNOCCHI AI 4 FORMAGGI

Melting gnocchi with Parmigiano, gorgonzola, ricotta and mozzarella.

PER 4 AMICI

For the gnocchi
- 1kg (2¼lb) good-quality potatoes
- 1 egg
- 350g (2½ cups) bread flour (Type 1 Italian flour)
- Salt QB

For the seasoning
- 400g (1¾ cups) Parmigiano fondue *(see page 288 for how to make your own)*
- 200g (7oz) gorgonzola
- 100g (3½oz) fior di latte (or mozzarella)
- 150g (½ cup) ricotta
- 150g (5½oz) Parmigiano Reggiano, grated

1
The gnocchi

Wash the potatoes, with their skins still intact. Put salted cold water in a saucepan, bring it to the boil and then add the potatoes, simmering them until they are ready (do not allow the water to come to the boil while they are cooking, as their skins could split). Drain the potatoes, then peel and mash them till smooth (don't swear! And avoid using a fork). Add the egg and flour, and knead the resulting dough by hand. Be fast as lightning here, so the potatoes don't cool down.

2
Roll this dough into sausages about 40cm (16in) long and 2cm (¾in) in diameter. Use a knife to cut them into gnocchi around 2cm (¾in) long. Put them in salted boiling water and cook until they rise to the surface. Drain them with a skimmer (if you don't have one, use a sieve – just get 'em outta the water) and transfer them to a bowl.

3
Now for the pièce de résistance

Add all the cheeses and the Parmigiano fondue to the gnocchi and mix. Transfer this mixture to an ovenproof dish or casserole and put under a medium grill for 15 minutes. Serve the gnocchi on a large plate, or straight from the dish. Enjoy – this dish is an absolute stunner.

A MINUTE TO SPARE?

Did you know that forks almost became obsolete after the fall of the Roman Empire? Legend has it that this piece of cutlery is now used practically all over the world only because Italians clung on to it to eat their pasta. You're welcome.

RISOTTO ALLO ZAFFERANO

Risotto milanese with saffron

PER 4 AMICI

- 420g (2 cups) Carnaroli, Vialone Nano, Roma or Baldo rice *(avoid precooked rice)*
- 140g (5oz) butter
- 120g (4oz) Parmigiano Reggiano, grated
- 1 shallot, chopped
- 50ml (3½ tbsp) white wine
- 800ml (3½ cups) vegetable stock
- 1g saffron strands

- Salt QB
- Pepper QB

For the gremolata
- 1 bunch sage
- Rosemary, finely chopped QB
- Zest of 1 lemon

1
Soften the shallot in 20g (¾oz) of butter in a saucepan. In the same saucepan, toast the rice for 2–3 minutes, stirring continuously (no skimping on this, otherwise the rice could burn). Deglaze with the white wine. Once this has evaporated, add the saffron, a pinch of salt and a little freshly ground pepper.

2
Pour in 200ml (¾ cup) of vegetable stock and stir. As soon as the liquid has evaporated, pour in another batch. Repeat this at least 2 more times. The rice should take around 15–17 minutes to cook, without ever burning or running out of liquid. Keep stirring all the time. Focus all your attention on the risotto – it will be worth the effort. Taste it and, once it's ready, add the Parmigiano and rest of the butter and then cover the risotto with a tea towel for 1½ minutes.

3
Meanwhile, stir the chopped rosemary with some freshly chopped sage leaves (not the stalks, as they're bitter) and mix them with the lemon zest. Uncover the risotto and stir vigorously. Serve the risotto on plates and delicately dress each with some of the gremolata. Now, what are you waiting for? Tuck in!

A MINUTE TO SPARE?

What should you do with any leftover rice? Store it then sauté it in a frying pan with some butter a few days later. Enrico's grandmother used to cook rice then reserve it expressly for this purpose. Try it out – you'll thank us for the tip.

GIANT RAVIOLO CARBONARA

XL carbonara ravioli with an oozing centre

PER 4 AMICI

- 400g (14oz) fresh pasta (*see how to make this really well on page 290*)
- 4 egg yolks (*keep the egg whites in the fridge and make some cute meringues using the recipe on page 306*)
- 80g (3oz) pecorino, grated
- 20g (¾oz) Parmigiano Reggiano, grated
- 150g (½ cup) ricotta
- 200g (7oz) guanciale
- Black pepper QB

1
  <u>Prepare the stuffing</u>
Mix the ricotta with 60g (2oz) of pecorino and 10g (⅓oz) of Parmigiano. Add a generous flurry of freshly ground pepper (this changes everything). Cut half the guanciale into matchsticks (*listarelle* in Italian) and brown them in a saucepan. Set aside, still in the pan. Once the guanciale matchsticks have cooled, add them to the cheese mixture.

2
  <u>Prepare the *ravioli*</u>
Roll out the pasta dough to obtain a sheet 2mm (¹/₁₀in) thick. Cut out 8 discs 18cm (7in) in diameter (you can use a bowl or a large mug, or even your kid's pencil pot, provided it's circular and the right size). Add a spoonful of stuffing to half the discs, about 7–8cm (2¾ –3in) in diameter.

3
  Sprinkle 10g (⅓oz) of Parmigiano on top, then add an egg yolk to the centre of the stuffing. Close the raviolo with another disc of pasta. Squeeze the edges together to ensure that they are closed tight. Put the raviolo in a saucepan of salted boiling water for 2½ minutes maximum (the egg yolk should be runny). Drain very very carefully in a sieve or with a slotted spoon, as it's a fragile little thing. Repeat this for the remaining 3 ravioli.

4
  <u>Looks are everything here</u>
If you want to be a top chef, try to avoid any cooking water going on the plates. Place the sieve on a tea towel before transferring the raviolo to a plate. Slice and brown the remaining guanciale in a frying pan and spoon it straight onto the ravioli, along with its fat (waste not, want not!). Sprinkle on the remaining 20g (¾oz) grated pecorino. If you're feeling fancy, you can grind some more fresh pepper on top – and there you are, *a tavola*!

A MINUTE TO SPARE?
Check your phone, you've probably left someone on 'read' and they're waiting for your reply.

TAGLIATELLE AI FUNGHI PORCINI

Tagliatelle with 3 mushrooms: porcini, oyster and button mushrooms

PER 4 AMICI

- 420g (1lb) fresh pasta *(you could even make this yourself by following our recipe on page 290)*
- 300g (11oz) ceps or porcini
- 100g (3½oz) button mushrooms
- 50g (1¾oz) oyster mushrooms
- 1 garlic clove, crushed

- 60g (2oz) butter
- ½ bunch thyme
- 4 tsp extra-virgin olive oil
- Salt QB
- Pepper QB

1 Let's start by all agreeing that porcini are the best mushrooms in the world. But it is also important to take advantage of Mother Nature's bounty and try more flavours, whilst being easy on the wallet. So we have no qualms with mixing it up with different types of shrooms. Variety is the spice of life.

2 Roll out the pasta dough to obtain a sheet 3mm (¹⁄₁₀ in) thick (this thickness is vital for texture and soaking up all the sauce). Fold it over 5 times (always in the same direction) then slice it horizontally with a knife in 1cm (⅓in) strips to obtain tagliatelle. Set aside.

3 Wipe off any dirt from the mushrooms with a damp cloth (don't wash them under a tap – they hate that!). Cut them into uniform slices. Heat the butter, thyme and garlic clove in a saucepan. Add the mushrooms and brown them over a high heat. Once they are cooked, remove the garlic.

4 Cook the tagliatelle in salted boiling water for 2–3 minutes (no more). Drain and add straight to the saucepan with the mushrooms and mix in the olive oil. Serve in pretty pasta bowls.

A MINUTE TO SPARE?

Our chef Albi absolutely adores Parmigiano. Accordingly, he uses it at every stage: in the recipe itself, as a seasoning, and when he plates. We'll let you decide whether you want to follow his example – you're the boss.

SPAGHETTI VONGOLE E BOTTARGA

Spaghetti with clams and bottarga

PER 4 AMICI

- 600g (1lb 5¼oz) spaghetti
- ½ kg (1lb 1½oz) clams (be sure to ask your fishmonger to clean them)
- 50g (1¾oz) bottarga
- 1 glass white wine (the first half goes into the pan, the second is for you to drink)

- 1 clove of garlic, crushed ('in camicia', as they say in Italy. For the uninitiated, this means 'with its shirt on', as the garlic clove is crushed with the skin still intact)
- 1 bunch of parsley (optional)
- Extra-virgin olive oil QB

1
Use a frying pan to sauté the garlic and clams in the oil for 4 minutes. Then add ½ glass of white wine.

2
If using the parsley, finely chop the stems (NB reserving the leaves), add and then cover the saucepan until the clams open. Take extra care to discard any clams that have not opened; we don't want you getting sick.

3
Put the spaghetti in a saucepan of salted boiling water until it is cooked al dente, then drain it roughly and add it to the clams. If some of the cooking water falls in along with the pasta, even better. Bravo, this will be *perfetto*! If you wish, add a few finely chopped parsley leaves, and then divide the pasta between 4 bowls. Just before serving, grate generous amounts of bottarga over each bowl, using a cheese grater. Enjoy *amici*!

A MINUTE TO SPARE?

We suggest that you avoid putting any Parmigiano on the table. Mixing fish and Parmigiano has been a sin for Italians ever since Hippocrates published his findings on nutrition in ancient times. He claimed that the digestion of cheese is very slow and could upset the digestion of any fish in the stomach. This notion has remained firmly lodged in the heads of Italians to this day. So, please, don't add anything. Just sit down and read a page of the dictionary.

THE GREAT LASAGNA

Or how to become your child's favourite.

PER 6 AMICI, AT LEAST
(although you can always invite fewer people and eat more)

- 600g (1lb 5¼oz) fresh pasta *(or sheets of dry pasta, if you don't have time to prepare the fresh version)*
- 800g (generous 3 cups) beef *ragù* *(see our recipe on page 298)*
- 250g (9oz) Parmigiano Reggiano, grated
- 70g (2½oz) butter

- 1 litre (1qt) cold whole milk
- 70g (½ cup) plain flour
- 1 pinch grated nutmeg
- Salt QB
- Pepper QB

1
Melt the butter in a saucepan. Add the flour and stir with a wooden spoon until you obtain a smooth paste. Leave to cook for 1 minute.

2
Without taking the pan off the heat, add the milk then whisk to eliminate any lumps. Add the nutmeg and allow the mixture to simmer for 3–4 minutes. Add salt and pepper then set the béchamel aside at room temperature, ready to be used later. Consult page 298 to find out how to make the *ragù*. Is it ready? Then, back to this recipe.

3
Roll out the pasta dough to obtain a sheet 3mm (¹⁄₁₀ in) thick, then cut it into sections matching the size of your baking dish. And what if they're too big to handle? In that case, cut them into 3 – you can stick them back together in the dish later on. Put your sheets of pasta into salted boiling water for 2 minutes then immerse them in a bowl of iced water for a further 2 minutes. Put a tea towel on the worktop, lay the pasta sheets on top and gently dry them. Skip this stage if you've opted for dry sheets – simply put them straight into the dish, without cooking them.

4
Give it some love, to make everything even more exquisite. Spread a thin layer of béchamel on the bottom. Cover this with pasta (as if you were spreading a miniature bedsheet). Mix the *ragù* with the rest of the bechamel and then fill the dish with a successives layers of pasta, *ragù* and, Parmigiano. Repeat this a maximum of 4 times, ending with Parmigiano on top.

5
Put the dish into the oven for 25–30 minutes, initially at 160°C fan/180°C/350°F/GM 4, for the first 20 minutes, then at 140°C fan/160°C/325°F/GM 3 for the final 10 minutes. If you think that the top of the lasagne is browning too quickly, cover it with a sheet of aluminium foil.

All done! Leave to rest for at least 20 minutes. It is very important to allow the lasagne to sit, otherwise it will turn into a soup. After that, it'll melt in the mouth and your kids will ask for an extra helping – mission accomplished!

A MINUTE TO SPARE?
It's a good time to check up on the plants on your balcony (or in the house). Are they thirsty?

A$AP GNOCCHI

Crunchy golden gnocchi

This is a typical Roman dish. Gnocchi means 'pieces of dough'. There are more than 20 types of gnocchi, and just as many variations in the flours and shapes used. Don't worry then that the ones here do not resemble the dumplings you are familiar with, as they all belong to the same happy family. Gnocchi is the frugal Italian way to use up all sorts of leftover dough (semolina, wheat, potato, polenta…).

PER 4 AMICI

- 250g (1½ cups) extra-fine semolina flour
- 1 litre (1qt) whole milk
- 200g (7oz) Parmigiano Reggiano, grated
- 110g (3¾oz) butter
- 2 egg yolks
- 1 pinch grated nutmeg
- Salt QB
- Pepper QB

1
Heat the milk in a saucepan. As soon as it's warm, add the salt, pepper and nutmeg. Once it begins to boil, gently pour in the semolina flour, whisking fast to avoid any lumps. Remove the saucepan from the heat and mix in 50g (1¾oz) of butter to get a smooth texture. Add 130g (4½oz) of Parmigiano and the egg yolks, beating vigorously with a wooden spoon.

2
Once the dough is smooth, spread it on a baking tray, in a sheet 4–5cm (1½–2in) thick, maximum. Leave to cool – this is a good time to walk the dog or hang out your laundry.

3
Once the dough has cooled, use any improvised pastry cutter with a diameter of around 10cm (it could be a glass or mug, a napkin holder…) and cut out as many circles as you can.

4
Place the gnocchi side by side in a large baking dish. Melt the remaining butter in a saucepan and pour it over the gnocchi. Sprinkle all the remaining Parmigiano on top and put the gnocchi under the grill in a convection oven at 230°C fan/250°C/480°F/GM 9 for 15–20 minutes.

5
Once the gnocchi are nicely golden brown, Gigi's mother usually serves them on a large plate on the table so that everybody can help themselves. It's up to you! For the record, she also puts a large sausage in the centre of the dish, which can only be eaten, if and only if, all the gnocchi are gone first. And as nobody has ever been able to finish this dish, the sausage is set aside for Sunday lunch. Manners maketh man.

A MINUTE TO SPARE?

This could be a good time to take out the rubbish. Don't forget to take your keys, as locking yourself out just before your guests arrive is a bit awkward.

5 TIPS ON CHOOSING GOOD DRIED PASTA

We can imagine that you don't always have time to make fresh pasta. So here are a few pointers on how to make the right decision on dried options, for a quick little pasta dish which everyone around the table will love.

1 If you see 'trafilata al bronzo' written on a packet of pasta, this means it has been 'bronze-cut', or traditionally made. This gives the pasta a texture to ensure the sauce clings to it, a guaranteed winner.

2 Check the origin of the wheat – it must come from Italy.

3 If the instructions on the packet specify a cooking time of more than 10 minutes, that may demand patience but it's a good sign nonetheless. The longer the pasta takes to cook, the better the quality. Any dried pasta that takes 2 minutes to cook is highly suspect.

4 Good Italian pasta on sale abroad will undoubtedly cost a little more than local rivals due to transportation costs, but you will definitely notice the difference on the plate.

5 Avoid dried egg pasta, even though it's extremely common, and opt as often as you can for pasta made from 100 per cent *semola di grano duro* (durum wheat flour). That's the ideal flour for authentic tagliatelle.

PIZZOCCHERI VALTELLINESI

Buckwheat pizzoccheri, potatoes, Bitto and kale:
the recipe that will turn you into a real Italian

PER 4 AMICI

- 500g (1lb 1½oz) *pizzoccheri* pasta *(available in all Italian delis)*
- 200g (7oz) kale
- 2 large potatoes

- 200g (7oz) butter
- 200g (7oz) Bitto cheese *(you should find this in the same deli as the pizzoccheri but, if not, go for Comté)*
- 5 or so sage leaves

---

1 Setting up

Pay attention, you're going to organize your kitchen like a real chef: wash the kale under a cold tap and then cut it into julienne strips. Set aside.

Peel the potatoes and dice them into 3cm (1in) cubes. Dice the cheese into 2cm (¾in) cubes. Set everything aside.

Melt the butter in a saucepan with the sage leaves until it turns a hazelnut colour. Then, turn off the heat. There you go, the preparations are complete, *bravo capo*.

2 Boil some salted water in a casserole dish or cast-iron pot, add the potatoes and cook them for 5 minutes. Add the *pizzoccheri* to the potatoes and cook for a further

7–8 minutes. Finally, add the kale and cook for a further 2 minutes. Drain the contents of the saucepan.

3 Put a third of this mixture straight back into the hot casserole dish, then spread on a layer of Bitto and spoon over a third of the browned butter. Repeat a further 2 times with the remaining mix. Make sure the cheese gets really melty, naughty and oozy (oh my!). Mix everything together, place on the table and stand back as the kids dive for the dish. *Splendido!* This treat is a popular Sunday meal in wintertime in Valtellina, Lombardy. Cosy.

A MINUTE TO SPARE?

Look up the Gardens of Bomarzo in Viterbo, Italy. Actually, we'll go even further, and tell you to book tickets to visit. Let us know how it went.

5 GOLDEN RULES FOR CHOOSING A GOOD PARMIGIANO

1
A good Parmigiano has been matured for at least 12 months.
The more mature, the better. Like wine
(or, let's face it, like people).

2
It must bear the name 'Parmigiano Reggiano', which will be
inscribed on the cheese's rind. Parmigiano can only be produced
exclusively between the provinces of Parma and Reggio Emilia.

3
Choose a Parmigiano Reggiano DOP – that way, you can be
sure that it's a true Parmigiano as its denomination
of origin is protected.

4
Buy Parmigiano in a chunk rather than as shavings or grated
in a packet, as these are often a mixture of different cheeses and
especially rind. They tend to have less flavour.

5
Can you see crystals in your Parmigiano?
These are neither salt crystals nor diamonds, but they do indicate
the passing of time – and that this cheese is *molto buono*!

ORECCHIETTE AL POMODORO

Orecchiette with fresh tomatoes, basil and ricotta salata

PER 4 AMICI

- 500g (1lb 1½oz) orecchiette
- 450ml (scant 2 cups) fresh tomato sauce *(you can also make your own using our recipe on page 300 – it will be even better that way)*
- 1 bunch basil

- 150g (5½oz) dry ricotta *(ricotta salata)* *(you will find this in an Italian deli – if not, buffalo mozzarella will do, but try the deli first)*
- Extra-virgin olive oil QB

1
Heat the tomato sauce in a saucepan over a low heat. Cook the orecchiette in salted boiling water until they are *al dente*. Drain them roughly with a slotted spoon and put them into the saucepan with the tomato sauce. The secret is to finish the pasta in the sauce, stirring all the while so it absorbs all the flavour.

2
Remove from the heat, add the basil leaves and a glug of the olive oil. Stir thoroughly and serve on a pretty plate in the middle of the table. At the last moment, grate the lovely ricotta atop.

All hail *Santa Ricotta!*

A MINUTE TO SPARE?

Empty the dishwasher. If it's dirty and full, turn it on; it would be a shame to have to put all your washing up in the sink overnight as there's no room.

SPAGHETTONE AI RICCI DI MARE

Spaghettone with sea urchins, garlic and olive oil

We are feeling generous, so we are going to give you 2 recipes in 1. A typical Italian recipe for knocking up when you get back home from work: *spaghettone aglio, olio, peperoncino*, and its bouji seafood version: *spaghettone aglio, olio, riccio di mare*. Is your mouth watering? Ours too.

PER 4 AMICI

- 600g (1¼lb) *spaghettone (following the recommendation of Charlotte, who is always hungry)*
- 150g (5½oz) sea urchins, minimum *(if you can't find any, ask your fishmonger to order and clean them for you)*

- 2 garlic cloves, chopped
- 1 fresh chilli, finely chopped
- 1 bunch flat-leaf parsley, finely chopped
- Extra-virgin olive oil QB

---

1 Put the pasta in a saucepan of salted boiling water and cook until *al dente*. Put a generous amount of olive oil in a large frying pan, along with the chilli and garlic, and brown them gently over a low heat for at least 6 minutes. Now you have 2 options, but whichever one you choose, be sure to keep all the oil. For real Italophiles, you can leave the chilli and garlic in the oil, or for newbies, you can sieve them out.

2 Add the pasta and a ladleful of the cooking water into the frying pan, along with the flavoured oil, and heat for 1 minute. Stir briskly so the water evaporates and creates a good emulsion. Cut open the sea urchins (watch out for the spikes!) and remove the 'tongues' (gonads) using a teaspoon. Add them to the saucepan, along with the parsley. Now is not the time to top up your drink – just sit down and get stuck in – *È pronto!* If you leave out the sea urchins, you will still have quintessential Italian comfort food. THE ultimate homecoming dish.

A MINUTE TO SPARE?

Fill up a carafe with tap water and pop it in the fridge. That way, you won't have the embarrassment of having only lukewarm water to offer your guests. It's even a good idea when you're on your own; you deserve the best.

CANNELLONI DELLA NONNA JAJA RICOTTA E SPINACI

Cannelloni stuffed with ricotta and spinach

PER 4 AMICI

- 16 cannelloni tubes *(they come in 1kg (2¼lb) packs – reckon on 4 tubes per person)*
- 400g (14oz) fresh spinach *(or frozen, which will work fine)*
- 1 egg
- 60g (¼ cup) cow ricotta
- 150g (5½oz) Parmigiano Reggiano, grated

- 300g (1⅓ cups) Parmigiano fondue *(see the wonderful recipe for a homemade version on page 288)*
- 1 pinch grated nutmeg
- Olive oil QB
- Salt QB
- Pepper QB

1
Put the cannelloni into a saucepan of salted boiling water for 3 minutes. Meanwhile, sauté the spinach in a saucepan with the olive oil. When it is cooked, chop it roughly with a knife.

2
Mix the spinach in a bowl with 30g (⅓ cup) of Parmigiano, the ricotta, the egg, the nutmeg, and some salt and pepper. Drain the cannelloni, dry them quickly with kitchen paper and stuff them with the spinach mixture.

3
Once all the tubes have been filled, carefully transfer them to a baking tray. Cover the cannelloni with the Parmigiano fondue, and spoil them even more by sprinkling grated Parmigiano on top and cook them for 15–20 minutes in an oven at 160°C fan/180°C/350°F/GM 4.

4
Serve 4 cannelloni on each plate – and now you're in for a treat. You'll never be able to take anybody seriously again who doesn't like spinach. Enjoy this dish like a true Italian, cutting and eating each cannelloni from one side to the other. That way you won't burn your mouth. See how we look out for you?

A MINUTE TO SPARE?

Find out which streaming platform is offering the film *Il Sorpasso (The Easy Life)* and make a vow to watch it very soon – it's a masterpiece.

SECONDI

BIG CAPRESE

Big caprese salad with fresh tomatoes, mozzarella and basil

PER 4 AMICI

- 4 buffalo mozzarellas (125g/4½oz each)
- 150g (generous 5oz) Datterini tomatoes
- 5 big heirloom tomatoes (*e.g. Green Zebra, Pineapple, Black Krim, for a wide range of colours*)
- 1 pinch brown sugar

- 1 bunch fresh basil (*really fresh, not that clump of wilting leaves lurking at the bottom of the fridge*)
- Extra-virgin olive oil QB
- Fior di sale QB
- Pepper QB

1
This, you'll see, is as simple as it's delicious. Chop the Datterini tomatoes in half and season them with olive oil, salt, pepper and brown sugar.

2
Place them on a baking tray and put them in an oven at 210°C fan/230°C/450°F/GM 8 for 4–5 minutes maximum. The tomatoes should be charred and blackened. Leave to cool.

3
Chop the heirloom tomatoes into quarters and season them with olive oil, basil, fior di sale, pepper and plenty of love. Mix the cooled charred tomatoes with the heirloom tomatoes. Add pieces of torn mozzarella.

4
Scatter plenty of basil leaves over the salad. And *buon appetito*!

A MINUTE TO SPARE?

Fancy going on a bigger journey tonight? You can always book a ticket (or 2, or 3…) for Verona. Apart from being the home of Romeo and Juliet, it's a delightful city with a maze of pretty backstreets. Verona is also close to Venice but, unlike its larger neighbour, receives far fewer visitors.

BUNNY & CLYDE

Rabbit stew with herbs, olives and toasted pine nuts

This rabbit recipe dates back to ancient times. It originates from Liguria, a crescent-shaped region in northwest Italy that's somewhat off the beaten track. It's a wonderfully tasty stew with herbs, olives, pine nuts and sometimes even tomato sauce. NB: this superb dish is likely to take rather more than 30 minutes of your time but, not to worry, as this *coniglio alla ligure* is truly sublime. Keep this recipe for a rainy Sunday, when you don't know what to do with yourself but fancy a really delicious meal. Another tip: before you start cooking, put 10 potatoes to roast in the oven with a drizzle of olive oil, some salt and pepper, and a sprig of rosemary. This perfect accompaniment to your stew will be ready at the same time as the rabbit. How's that for planning?

PER 4 AMICI

- 1kg (2¼lb) rabbit (*ask your butcher for various cuts, so you get a range of textures*)
- 1 white onion, finely chopped
- 1 garlic clove, finely chopped
- 80g (scant ½ cup) Taggiasche olives
- 20g (3 tbsp) pine nuts, toasted
- 1 glass red wine

- ½ bunch thyme
- 1 sprig rosemary
- 2 bay leaves
- 300ml (1¼ cups) extra-virgin olive oil
- Coarse salt QB

1
Chop the rabbit roughly to obtain 10–12 pieces. Heat the olive oil in a deep cast-iron pan or casserole dish. Add the garlic and onion.

2
Add the meat. When all the pieces are browned, add some salt and deglaze in the red wine. Leave to evaporate for 3–4 minutes – meanwhile, pour yourself a drink too, *cin cin!*

3
Add the herbs, cook for a further 3 minutes then add the olives and pine nuts.

4
Add 200ml (generous ¾ cup) of lukewarm water (not boiling) and pour it over the rabbit. Partially cover the saucepan and allow its contents to simmer for at least 40 minutes over a very low heat. Do not cover completely as the liquid needs to reduce. Then, tuck in – and allow time afterwards for a brief siesta so you can digest this feast, or at least ruminate on the wonderful meal you prepared with such masterly skill.

A MINUTE TO SPARE?
Listen (or jive) to Mina's classic 'Tintarella di luna'.

9 COOL ITALIAN FACTS

1 Italy boasts more varieties of pasta than all the saucepans in your kitchen. There are more than 140 types of pasta, with names that can vary from one region to the next.

2 There are over 50 UNESCO World Heritage Sites dotted across the Boot – more than any other country. They range from the Castel del Monte in Puglia to the Basilica of St Francis of Assisi and the entire historic centre of Naples.

3 Italians never drink cappuccino after 10am. Obviously, they order coffee after the *colazione*, but it has to be drunk neat, and never as a takeaway. Real Italians drink it standing up, at the counter.

4 Family is the most important thing in the world, without question. And our Mamma, in particular, comes before any fling, partner or friend. Mamma knows best!

5 Don't be alarmed if you hear a car horn blasting away once or twice, or even 34 times in a row, when you're in Naples. You're not necessarily being alerted to an imminent danger. Far more likely it will be a driver greeting a friend on the other side of the street. It's a very common practice. Keep your eyes peeled though, as maybe they're saying hi to you!

6 Italy has the oldest university in Europe, in Bologna (1088). Brush up your Latin before your next dinner – it may be a dead language but it also happens to be very cool.

7 The 3 most active volcanoes in Europe are all in Italy: Etna, Vesuvius and Stromboli. This explains why all our chefs are so hot-blooded.

8 The word *'mozzarella'* comes from the Neapolitan dialect. It is derived from the verb *'mozzare'*, which means 'to cut and knead curds'. You can try this fun fact out on your next date, *di niente*.

9 The Romans love cats so much that they are part of the city's cultural legacy. All felines are protected by law, with them being the only inhabitants of Rome authorized to live in the ancient ruins. How purrfect!

FRITTAVENTURA

A big platter of little fried fish

PER 4 AMICI

For the seafood
- 1st choice: go to the fishmonger's and ask for the freshest shellfish and small fry available (*red mullet, anchovies, cuttlefish, prawns, etc.*)
- 2nd choice: 1kg (2¼lb) squid

For the batter
- 500g (3½ cups) semolina flour
- 1 lemon
- Sunflower oil QB
- Salt QB

1
If you're using whole squid, first pull out the tentacles, remove the beak, then wash the squid under cold water. Roughly slice the body and chop the tentacles into pieces.

2
If you are buying a mixture from the fishmonger's, ask them to clean everything. Don't bother chopping the smallest fish, as they make a perfect mouthful just as they are.

3
Heat a generous amount of sunflower oil in a heavy-bottomed saucepan. Put the semolina flour into a bowl, add the seafood and mix. When the oil in the saucepan is piping hot (around 170°C/340°F), immerse the fish and deep-fry them for 3 minutes until they are crispy and brown. Try to avoid getting splashed by the hot oil.

4
Transfer the fish to a sheet of kitchen paper to absorb any excess fat, before serving them in the middle of the table. Squeeze on some lemon juice and sprinkle with a pinch of salt. NB: never cover your little fish and avoid piling them on top of each other, as this will make them go soft. This is unthinkable, especially once they inevitably become the family favourite.

A MINUTE TO SPARE?

We recommend keeping a pot of aïoli to hand. Make the most of these little treasures by dunking them in aioli (or even mayonnaise) and washing them down with a little glass of prosecco.

COTOLETTE ALLA BOLOGNESE

Bolognese-breaded veal chops (nothing to do with the sauce from the same city)

- 4 veal cutlets (around 200g/7oz per slice)
- 300g (11oz) Prosciutto di Parma, sliced
- 200g (7oz) Parmigiano Reggiano, grated
- 3 whole eggs
- 100g (⅔ cup) plain flour
- 300g (2 cups) breadcrumbs
- 250ml (1 cup) sunflower oil

For the stock
- 600g (1lb 5¼oz) chicken carcass (*ask your butcher – it will cost you practically nothing*)
- 1 carrot
- 1 white onion
- 1 stalk celery
- Peppercorns QB

1
Put all the ingredients for the stock into a saucepan and cover them completely with cold water. Simmer for around 1 hour, without ever allowing the water to come to the boil. Then, turn off the heat, leave to cool and strain the liquid. Friendly reminder: strain with a ladle and a sieve, to ensure that all the sediment remains at the bottom of the saucepan and does not taint the stock.

2
Spread the pieces of meat on the worktop and flatten them with a meat tenderizer (e.g., a rolling pin, or that enormous dictionary that's been gathering dust ever since you've had a smartphone) so that each slice is 1cm thick.

3
Dip each slice into the flour, then into the egg and, finally, into the breadcrumbs. Pour plenty of sunflower oil into a frying pan and deep-fry the slices of veal. Then, transfer them to a sauté pan (or another frying pan).

4
Add Prosciutto di Parma to the top of each cutlet then liberally sprinkle with Parmigiano. Pour in the stock around the sides of the pan (to avoid disturbing the toppings). Simmer, covered, for 5–6 minutes maximum. Now it's ready to eat!

We like to serve these cutlets with baked potatoes, but that's entirely up to you. Life is what you make of it.

A MINUTE TO SPARE?

Make some room for the coats, bags and (even) helmets that your guests will probably bring with them. Clear out a cupboard, leave some space on the bed… anything than having to cook surrounded by clutter.

NO FIG DEAL

Fig, mozzarella and Prosciutto di Parma salad

PER 4 AMICI

- 300g (11oz) Prosciutto di Parma *(preferably cut into thin slices by your* salumiere, *as a deli worker is known in Italy)*
- 4 buffalo mozzarellas (125g/4½oz each)
- 200g (7oz) fresh figs (or substitute with melon)
- Salt QB
- Pepper QB

- Extra-virgin olive oil QB
- Basil QB

1 Roughly tear the mozzarellas into pieces and arrange them on a large plate. Add bits of Prosciutto di Parma here and there (we're relying on you to create something on a par with a Picasso here). Cut the figs into 4 and spread them on top.

2 Make it rain with basil leaves, salt and pepper, then drizzle on a healthy glug of plenty of olive oil – now, get to the table, dinner's ready!

3 In Italy, this salad is typically eaten on toasted slices of sourdough bread. A salad that will bring the sunshine right through to October.

A MINUTE TO SPARE?

Put 'Rumore' by Raffaella Carrà on in the background. Nothing can possibly go wrong after that.

SCALOPPINE DELLA MAMMA

Veal escalope with Fontina and ham

For the meat...
• Ideally use 880g (2lb) cushion of veal, if not consult your butcher, or use topside beef

For the rest...
• 8 slices of cooked ham *(reckon on 40g/1½oz per slice)*
• 8 hearty slices of Fontina *(an Italian cheese produced in the Aosta Valley, just near the border with France; If you can't find it, 350g/¾lb Comté will do the job)*
• 60g (2oz) butter

• Plain flour QB
• 1 glass dryish white wine
• Salt QB
• Pepper QB

1   Put the flour, salt and pepper in a bowl and coat the veal in this mixture.

2   Melt the butter in a frying pan and brown the pieces of veal on both sides. Add the white wine to deglaze the pan. Put a layer of ham on top of each escalope, followed by a layer of Fontina (or Comté). Cover the frying pan so it melts.

3   Once the cheese has melted, remove the *scaloppine* from the pan. Serve these little delights with a silky smooth mashed potato – we hope to hear you raving about it.

A MINUTE TO SPARE?

Discreetly leave a few pairs of cosy slippers by the front door. It's a subtle way of hinting to your guests that they should take off their shoes, without saying so outright.

10 MUST-TRY ITALIAN WINES

1 BRUNELLO DI MONTALCINO

A great wine from Tuscany produced under the DOCG classification ('controlled and guaranteed designation of origin' in English). This high-quality cru dates back centuries! Perfect for red meats and pecorino.

2 BAROLO
All hail the king! A sublime red from Piedmont made with the Nebbiolo grape. It's ideal for a royal banquet of steak, slow-cooked meat and game.

3 AMARONE DELLA VALPOLICELLA

A dry red wine from Verona that boasts a DOCG classification. The name 'Amarone' derives from the word *amaro*, meaning 'bitter', as the gifted winemaker behind its creation had initially intended to make a sweet wine, not something so delicious it'll have you whispering sweet nothings.

4 BARBARESCO
This has a deep, intense colour, set off by a fruity aroma with a tinge of violet and spicy notes.

5 BOLGHERI DOC
A wine made with a Bordeaux-blend of grape varieties. Made in vineyards next to the Mediterranean with a beautiful sea breeze.

6 MONTEPULCIANO D'ABRUZZO

One of the first DOC wines in Italy. Once aged, it makes a good match for goat's cheese.

7 AGLIANICO
Made from one of the oldest varieties of grapes in Italy. This grape has been living it's best life in the sun, giving it a great complexity of aromas and flavours

8 PRIMITIVO
The name, from the Latin *primitivus*, or 'first', alludes to the date of its harvest – in August, before all the other grapes.

9 PINOT GRIGIO
A greyish-blue colour of grape with a characteristic elegance and flavour profile. Round, with a long finish, with complex woody flavours that can be slightly smoky or flowery.

10 PECORINO
This grape from Latium, in central Italy, is a very old variety. Its name is derived from the Italian word *pecora*, meaning 'sheep', as it grows in mountains where sheep graze.

POLPO PICASSO

Neapolitan octopus with olives, capers and Datterini tomatoes

PER 4 AMICI
(invite whoever you want – after a good meal, everybody's a friend)

- 1 whole octopus
- 100g (generous 1 cup) Taggiasche olives
- 100g (¾ cup) capers preserved in salt
- 500g (1lb 1½oz) San Marzano tomatoes, canned
- 300g (11oz) Datterini tomatoes
- 1 shallot, finely chopped

- 1 glass red wine (*the first half goes in the recipe, the second is for you*)
- ½ bunch basil
- Extra-virgin olive oil QB
- Salt QB
- Pepper QB

1
Roughly chop the octopus. Heat some oil in a saucepan and add the octopus pieces, along with the shallot. Add the olives, capers and sprigs of basil.

2
Pour in half a glass of red wine to deglaze the mixture. Drink the rest of the wine (down the hatch!). Put both tomatoes in a saucepan, season with salt and pepper, and simmer for around 35 minutes.

3
When the tomatoes have reduced and the octopus looks juicy, transfer both to a nicely warmed serving dish (preferably with a lid, to retain the heat).

4
We like to serve steamed potatoes on the side. This octopus will change your life – or at least your dinner.

A MINUTE TO SPARE?

If you've already had your shower and the meal is almost ready, start tidying up the bits and bobs left out around your kitchen. A tedious job, maybe, but you'll be glad it's done.

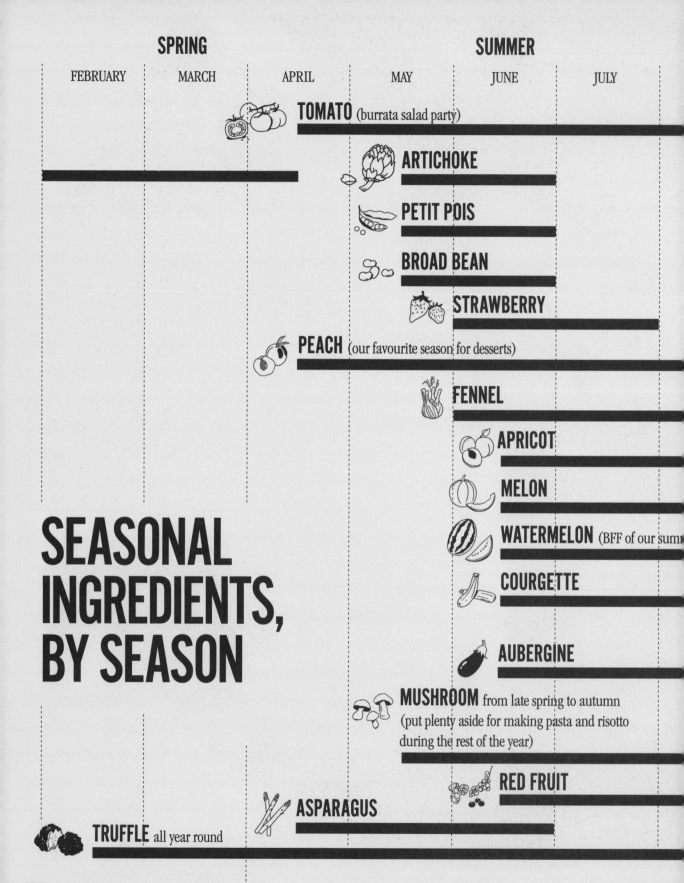

SEASONAL INGREDIENTS, BY SEASON

SPRING

FEBRUARY   MARCH   APRIL   MAY

SUMMER

JUNE   JULY

TOMATO (burrata salad party)

ARTICHOKE

PETIT POIS

BROAD BEAN

STRAWBERRY

PEACH (our favourite season for desserts)

FENNEL

APRICOT

MELON

WATERMELON (BFF of our sum

COURGETTE

AUBERGINE

MUSHROOM from late spring to autumn (put plenty aside for making pasta and risotto during the rest of the year)

RED FRUIT

ASPARAGUS

TRUFFLE all year round

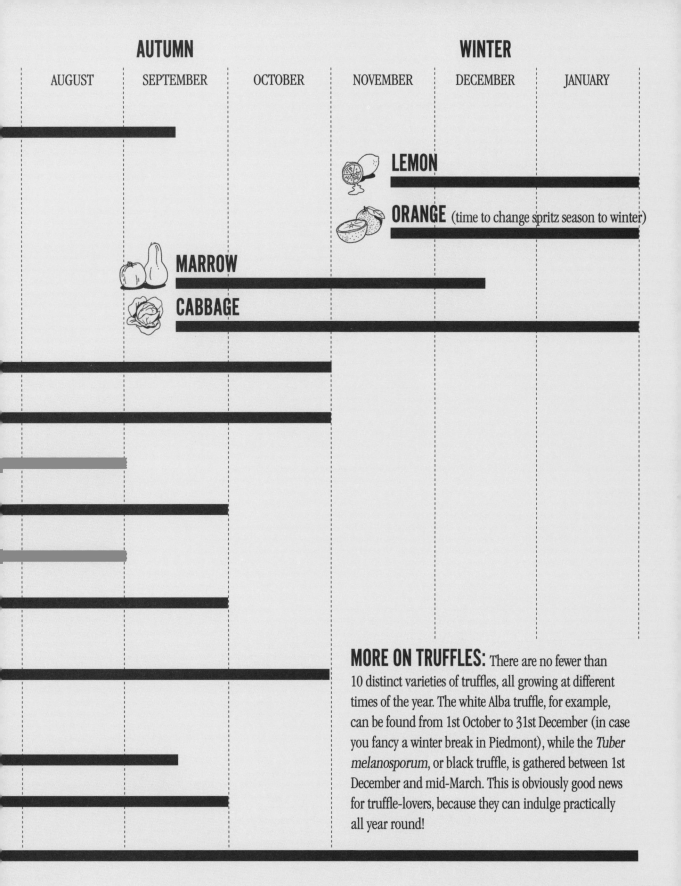

AUTUMN

AUGUST · SEPTEMBER · OCTOBER

WINTER

NOVEMBER · DECEMBER · JANUARY

LEMON

ORANGE (time to change spritz season to winter)

MARROW

CABBAGE

MORE ON TRUFFLES: There are no fewer than 10 distinct varieties of truffles, all growing at different times of the year. The white Alba truffle, for example, can be found from 1st October to 31st December (in case you fancy a winter break in Piedmont), while the *Tuber melanosporum*, or black truffle, is gathered between 1st December and mid-March. This is obviously good news for truffle-lovers, because they can indulge practically all year round!

BIG VEGGIE KEBABS

Edo's one and only recipe for vegetarian kebabs

A treat dreamed up by Edoardo, our wonderful chef with 1001 vegetarian recipes up his sleeve. We are so thrilled to share this recipe with you, so hopefully you'll be inspired to give pride of place to vegetables. This dish can be prepared in the oven in winter, or on a barbecue with seasonal vegetables in summer (a refreshing change from burgers no?).

PER 2 AMICI

- 2 smoked mozzarellas (provola or scamorza)
- 2 Jerusalem artichokes
- 1 pak choi
- 1 red onion, peeled
- 1 pinch sugar
- 1 tsp cider vinegar

For the sauce
- 100g (6 tbsp) miso
- 2 heads of garlic, peeled and with the middle sprout removed
- Milk QB
- 1 tsp cider vinegar
- 100ml (7 tbsp) extra-virgin olive oil
- Salt QB
- Pepper QB

1
Wash all the vegetables and chop them into pieces, roughly equal in size. You now have 2 options.

Option 1
For real pros, there's a different cooking method for each of your 3 main ingredients. Blanch the Jerusalem artichokes in a saucepan of milk for 5 minutes (reserve the milk afterwards, as it will come in handy for the sauce). Brown the onion in a frying pan with the cider vinegar and the sugar. You want it to take on a nice caramel colour. Meanwhile, blanch the pak choi in a saucepan of salted boiling water. Don't forget to season everything with salt and pepper!

Option 2
If you're pushed for time, blanch the Jerusalem artichoke, onion and pak choi together in salted boiling water.

2
Whichever option you choose: once the 3 main ingredients are cooked, skewer them in alternating layers, plus a piece of mozzarella after every 3 vegetables. Season with salt and pepper.

3
For the sauce
Gently brown the 2 heads of garlic in milk (use the milk left over from cooking the Jerusalem artichokes, if you chose option 1) until they are soft. Heat the olive oil with the miso in a saucepan, cook over a high heat and then add the garlic, retaining the milk for later. Turn off the heat, add the cider vinegar and gently combine all the ingredients with a hand blender. Gradually incorporate the milk, while continuing to blend the sauce. Once you have obtained a good consistency, transfer the sauce to a small bowl, place it in the centre of the table and everything is ready for a 100% veg-filled feast. What can beat that?

A minute to spare?

Check on any forthcoming photography exhibitions in your area. Wouldn't it be great to see some proper photos, rather than those that pop up on your smartphone?

JULIUS CAESAR

Eric's famous Caesar salad, the ultimate summer meal

PER 4 AMICI

- 4 fillets of chicken
- 1 garlic clove, finely chopped
- 4 hearts of Romaine lettuce
- 200g (7oz) button mushrooms
- 2 anchovy fillets in brine
  (or in oil, if that is all you have)
- 35g (4 tbsp) capers in brine
- 100g (⅔ cup) plain flour
- 100g (1 cup) panko breadcrumbs (if not, homemade breadcrumbs will do just fine)

- 4 eggs
- 60g (7 tbsp) Parmigiano Reggiano, grated
- 1tsp Worcester sauce
- Espelette pepper QB
- 250ml (1 cup) sunflower oil (or olive oil or grapeseed oil)
- 250ml (1 cup) extra-virgin olive oil
- Fine salt QB
- Black pepper QB
- 1 tsp white wine vinegar

1 Caesar dressing

Separate the whites and yolks of the 3 eggs (put the whites aside to make some great meringues, using the recipe on page 306). Put the yolks in a bowl and add the vinegar, salt and pepper. Gradually whisk in equal amounts of olive oil and sunflower oil (setting aside 20ml/4 tsp of the latter for the frying stage) to create a light, creamy sauce. Combine a third of this mayonnaise with the garlic, half the capers and all the anchovies, then gradually incorporate the rest of the dressing. Add the Worcester sauce. Finally, add Espelette pepper and set aside.

2 Breaded chicken

Arrange 3 different bowls containing, respectively, a little flour, the remaining egg whisked and some panko breadcrumbs. Dip the chicken fillets in each bowl, in the above order. Brown the chicken pieces in a frying pan with the reserved sunflower oil, which should be piping hot. Be careful not to burn your fingers. If you're a stickler for detail, you can brown the fillets in clarified butter in a frying pan and, if necessary, finish off cooking them in the oven. It's up to you, depending on how much time you have.

3 The salad

Lightly brown the remaining breadcrumbs in the oven at 120°C fan/140°C/285°F/GM 1 for 20 minutes. Meanwhile, wash the remaining capers to eliminate the brine. Dry them and then fry in hot oil. Cut the lettuce hearts into chunks 2cm (¾ in) thick. Finely chop the capers, then peel the mushrooms and chop them into 1cm (⅓ in) dice.

4 The presentation

Repeat the following 4 times over, using your most beautiful plates. Place a chunk of lettuce in the centre and then coat them in some of the Caesar dressing. Cut the chicken fillets into 5mm-wide (⅙ in) strips and arrange a quarter of them on your bed of lettuce. Add a further layer of lettuce, along with another layer of the dressing. Sprinkle some of the finely chopped lettuce leaves on top and scatter some diced mushroom around the base of the salad. Put any remaining Caesar dressing into a piping bag. Pipe the dressing over each plate with as much pizzazz as you can muster (the secret of this recipe lies partly in the presentation, so give it your all! Go on, we believe in you!). Finish with the capers, the toasted panko breadcrumbs and an avalanche of Parmigiano – and your masterpiece is complete, ready for the table. *chef kiss*

A MINUTE TO SPARE?

You can reflect on how best to greet the guests who are about to turn up. With kisses? Or without? Best to establish the ground rules before they arrive.

CONTORNI

POWER TO THE CAULIFLOWER

Insanely good cauliflower in Parmigiano cheese sauce.

- 2 cauliflowers
- 100g (½ cup) Parmigiano fondue (*see the wonderful recipe for a homemade version on page 298*)
- 100g (3½oz) Parmigiano Reggiano, grated
- 70g (5 tbsp) butter
- 70g (½ cup) plain flour

- 1 litre (1qt) cold whole milk
- 1 dash white vinegar
- 1 pinch grated nutmeg
- Salt QB
- Pepper QB

1
Wash the cauliflowers under cold water. Cut off their stems then blanch the florets in salted boiling water plus the dash of vinegar, for a maximum of 1–2 minutes. You want the cauliflower to still have a bite, so the flavours really pop.

2
For the béchamel
Melt the butter in a saucepan. Add the flour and then stir with a wooden spoon to obtain a smooth paste. Leave to simmer for 1 minute. Add the cold milk to the saucepan (while still on the heat), then beat the mixture to avoid any lumps. Add the nutmeg and simmer for 3–4 minutes. Season with salt and pepper.

3
Combine the béchamel with the Parmigiano fondue. Arrange the cauliflower florets in a baking dish, cover them with the sauce, sprinkle on the Parmigiano and transfer the dish to an oven heated to 160°C fan/180°C/350°F/GM 4, for 15 minutes maximum. And there you are! Done and dusted, *baci baci*.

We like to put the dish on the table so everyone can help themselves. Cheesy cauliflower tastes even better when you've had to fight people off to get it on your plate.

A MINUTE TO SPARE?

Hurry out and buy a soft drink for your guests who don't drink alcohol. It always feels like a bit of a punishment to be offered only a glass of water in place of wine.

CAPONATA GOALS

A Sicilian's recipe for caponata

PER 4 AMICI

- 800g (1¾lb) aubergines
- 200g (7oz) white onions
- 800g (1¾lb) courgettes
- 200g (7oz) Datterini tomatoes
- 100g (3½oz) vine ripened tomatoes
- 40g (5 tbsp) capers preserved in coarse salt
- 200g *(generous 1 cup)* green olives, pitted and preserved in brine
- 40g (⅓ cup) pine nuts, toasted

- 50g (3½ tbsp) white sugar
- Basil QB
- 40ml (2½ tbsp) white wine vinegar
- Sunflower oil QB
- Extra-virgin olive oil QB
- Salt QB
- Pepper QB

1
Slice the onions into julienne strips. Chop the aubergines, courgettes and the vine ripened tomatoes into 3cm cubes. Cut the olives into 2.

2
In a saucepan, simmer the onions, capers, courgettes and olives in olive oil. Add 20g (1½ tbsp) sugar, the Datterini and vine ripened tomatoes, and the pine nuts. Simmer for a further 20 minutes.

3
Fry the aubergines in a heavy-bottomed saucepan with piping-hot sunflower oil for 3–4 minutes. Add the vegetables from the other saucepan, along with the vinegar and the rest of the sugar. Stir. Add salt and freshly ground pepper. Turn up the heat in order to caramelize the sugar and evaporate the vinegar. Allow this to simmer for 5 minutes whilst stirring, so you get a lovely caramelized flavour.

4
Turn off the heat and add the basil leaves (wash them under cold water first) and leave to cool (ideally on the balcony, but never in the fridge).

Serve the caponata as we would at home in Italy: put it in a large serving dish and let everybody help themselves – it tastes even better that way. *Bravo, capo.*

A MINUTE TO SPARE?

Listen to the podcast 'Stuff You Should Know' to expand your mind as you cook.

ZUCCHINE ALLA SCAPECE

Neapolitan-style grilled courgettes

PER 4 AMICI

- 4 courgettes
- 2 garlic cloves, chopped
- A few basil leaves, finely chopped
- A few mint leaves, finely chopped
- 50ml (3½ tbsp) white wine vinegar

- Sunflower oil QB (*as in the words our beloved chef Giuseppe's nonna: 'if it's fried, it's good'*)
- 100ml (7 tbsp) extra-virgin olive oil
- Salt QB
- Pepper QB

1
Slice your courgettes into pieces about the thickness of a pound or dollar coin. Gradually transfer all the pieces to a heavy-bottomed saucepan with piping-hot oil and sauté them until they take on a nice golden-brown colour.

2
Meanwhile, mix together the chopped mint and basil leaves in a salad bowl and add 20ml (4 tsp) olive oil. Add the garlic cloves, the white wine vinegar, pepper and salt (just a little), stir again and and toss in the courgettes.

3
Leave these guys to rest for 15–20 minutes – enough time to spruce yourself up before your guests arrive. Or to reward yourself with a drink. Finally, gather around the table to share this salad brimming with love.

A MINUTE TO SPARE?

The Instagram account @filmthusiast is guaranteed to get you into a good mood. It might even provide some topics of conversation for the dinner table.

WHAT MAKES A GOOD HAM

1 Generally speaking, the more mature, the better! But the most important thing is to trust your own taste buds. Personally, we prefer a maturing period of at least 24 months.

2 DOP ham: Parma, San Daniele… when a ham is DOP, it means it has benefitted from well-chosen raw materials, an optimal maturing technique and a manufacturing process that has taken place entirely in Italy.

3 Ham should have the right colour. Your slices of ham should be neither too pale (which means it's not mature enough) nor too dark. The balance between fat and meat is another factor to take into account. Too much fat is a problem – but too little is a bad sign as well. Specks of tyrosine (in the form of little white dots) are another indication of quality.

4 Good ham can be found everywhere: keep your eyes peeled (and make sure you don't get ripped off!). The best hams are not necessarily the most expensive, and they can often be found in unassuming shops.

5 A good ham must come from and be made in Italy. You can't find an Italian ham? Well, at least make sure that the ham has a good provenance and has been ethically sourced. Beware of any spelling mistakes on the labelling – they're a pretty sure sign of a scam.

MELANZANE SOTT'OLIO

Melt-in-the-mouth aubergines in olive oil

PER 4 AMICI

- 4 aubergines
- 2 garlic cloves, finely chopped
- 1 fresh chilli, finely chopped
- 1 bunch flat-leaf parsley, finely chopped
- A few mint leaves, finely chopped
- 60ml (¼ cup) (at least) extra-virgin olive oil
- Salt QB
- Pepper QB

---

1   SPOILER ALERT: it is important to finish this dish around an hour before serving. That gives you time to run yourself a nice hot bath instead of your usual quick shower. Get out the bubbles!

2   Chop the aubergines into slices around 5mm (⅛in) thick. Sear them in a hot dry frying pan for around 3 minutes on each side, until they are nice and brown.

3   Combine the olive oil, chilli, mint, parsley and garlic in a bowl. Add the aubergines and toss everything together. Season with salt and pepper and leave the dish to rest for a good hour. For optimum results, make sure the oil completely covers the aubergines. A bit of oil never hurt nobody!

Finally, place the dish in the middle of the table, summon your guests and get stuck in.

A MINUTE TO SPARE?

You can use it to check what's on at your local museums. It is good to get up close and personal with works of art occasionally.

MELANZANE A FUNGHETTO

Fried aubergines with garlic and caramelized tomatoes

PER 4 AMICI

- 3 large aubergines *(you may have some leftovers for the next day)*
- 500g (1lb 1½oz) Datterini tomatoes
- 1 garlic clove, crushed
- ½ bunch basil
- Extra-virgin olive oil QB
- Salt QB

1 Dice the aubergines and fry them, along with half the garlic clove, in a frying pan with plenty of olive oil for at least 10 minutes. Meanwhile, put some more oil in a frying pan to caramelize the Datterini tomatoes, along with the other half of the garlic clove, for 5 minutes maximum.

2 Once the ingredients are cooked, combine them in a bowl with a little salt and pepper and a few basil leaves. Mix thoroughly. And there you are – all done!

If there are any leftovers, we like to put them in a sandwich the next day or spread them over a pizza for supper. We love it veggie veggie much.

A MINUTE TO SPARE?

Have relatives visiting this evening? Then it's time to dig out all the unused presents they've given you. Just think how pleased your mother-in-law will be to see her gift on the side table.

CIPOLLINE BORETTANE

Caramelized onions

We're crazy about these little onions. Italians eat them as a starter with focaccia and slices of cooked meat. They're a knockout.

PER 4 AMICI

- 700g (1½lb) *cipolline* (pearl/button onions), outer skin removed
- 35g (generous 2 tbsp) butter
- 45g (3 tbsp) brown sugar
- 200ml (generous ¾ cup) water
- 45ml (3 tbsp) cider vinegar
- 1 sprig of thyme
- 1 bay leaf
- Salt QB
- Peppercorns QB

1 Melt the brown sugar in a saucepan over a low heat. Add the butter then the onions. Season with salt and pepper, then brown the onions over a high heat for 2–3 minutes.

2 Deglaze with the vinegar then add the thyme and bay leaf. When the vinegar starts to evaporate, gradually add water and leave the onions to simmer, covered, over a low heat for around 30 minutes. When the onions are thoroughly caramelized and ready to eat, transfer them to a bowl and take it straight to the table. They're epic!

A MINUTE TO SPARE?

Get your children dressed up in their new clothes. No children? Well, then you know what to do... #haveaquickie

PATATE AL FORNO

Soon to be your favourite roast potatoes of all time

PER 4 AMICI

- 1kg (2¼lb) potatoes
- Vinegar QB
- Sunflower oil QB
- Extra-virgin olive oil QB

- Fresh sorrel, finely chopped QB *(optional)*
- Salt QB
- Pepper QB

1 Wash the potatoes under cold water and slice them lengthwise, without peeling. It's precisely the rough skin that gives the beloved potato all its texture and flavour.

Little fact, in Italy potatoes sliced in this way are called *spicchi*, meaning small pieces, but of course you Brits have a more obvious word… 'wedges'.

2 Blanch the potatoes in a saucepan of water with salt and vinegar for 1½ minutes. Then transfer them to an oven tray and liberally drizzle on both olive oil and sunflower oil. Mix thoroughly. Add coarse salt and pepper, and then roast the potatoes in the oven for 25 minutes at 190°C fan/210°C/410°F/GM 6. Halfway through the roasting process, turn all the *patatine* the other way round. Once the potatoes are cooked, remove them from the oven. Now is the time, if you wish, to follow Lorenzo's recommendation to add a little fresh sorrel on top as garnish.

In Italy, people put the roasting tray straight on the table, to avoid having to wash up too many dishes. There's another reason, however — the real fun here lies in scooping up all the crispy bits on the bottom of the roasting tray.

A MINUTE TO SPARE?

Get hold of the film *Once Upon a Time in America* and treat yourself to a cinema session. It's an American masterpiece… by an Italian director.

5 PLACES IN ITALY TO ADD TO YOUR BUCKET LIST

1 The Diego Armando Maradona Stadium in Naples. This was renamed in 2020, following the great man's death. Maradona displayed his skills here for a full 7 years to the delight of the local fans.

2 The Spiaggia Rosa (Pink Beach) on Budelli. The sand here is naturally pink, set off by transparent blue water. This little corner of paradise is now a protected area: visitors can look at the beach but are forbidden to walk on it.

3 Il Duomo di Milano (the Milan Dome). This is the third biggest cathedral in the world but nothing can prepare you for its amazing rooftop terrace with a panoramic view of the city, with the Alps in the background. This is Milan, baby.

4 Faraglioni di Capri: this is our own gorgeous little getaway. The sheer, chalky cliffs and 3 imposing sea stacks to the south-east of the island are utterly breathtaking. This trio even have names: Stella, Saetta and Scopolo. *Che carino*!

5 The view from Chef Monia's mamma's home in Procida. Even if you don't make it to this loving home, you can still wander around the marvellous island.

PEPERONI AL FORNO MARINATI

Marinated red peppers

PER 4 AMICI

- 4 large red peppers
- 1 garlic clove, finely chopped
- ½ bunch basil

- 70ml (5 tbsp) extra-virgin olive oil
- Salt QB
- Pepper QB

1
Lay the peppers, whole, on a baking tray and roast them for 15 minutes at 230°C fan/250°C/480°F/GM 9, or as high as your oven will go. Turn them over halfway through and make sure they don't burn. They should turn black, though, so don't panic!

2
Once they are thoroughly cooked, transfer them to a plastic container, put the lid on and set aside for 20 minutes at room temperature. Now's the time to do something else: open a good bottle of wine or finish tidying up before your guests arrive.

3
After this little break, remove the peppers' skins and seeds, break them up roughly with your hands, transfer them to a large dish and cover all the pieces with garlic and olive oil. Don't forget to season with salt and pepper. The longer you leave the peppers to marinate, the tastier they will be. As Alberto never tires of telling us, good food is made with love and patience. In Italy, peppers can even end up being marinated in the fridge for 3 whole days. Love lasts for 3 days. So, don't think twice about waiting a few hours before eating them. Just before serving, garnish with the basil.

A MINUTE TO SPARE?

If there happens to be any leftovers, these delicious peppers can be used in various ways: in a panino with meat, alongside some mozzarella, or to add some extra oomph to a spicy mayonnaise. You will love this one: blend the peppers with a little warm water to obtain a stunning dip to serve as a snack alongside freshly baked bread or breadsticks.

FUNGHI TOWN

Fricassee of assorted mushrooms

PER 4 AMICI

- 900g (2lb) assorted mushrooms (*button and oyster mushrooms, ceps, black trumpet, girolles, etc. Be creative but avoid anything that's not legal*)
- 1 garlic clove, finely chopped
- 30g (2 tbsp) butter

- A few thyme leaves
- Extra-virgin olive oil QB
- Salt QB
- Pepper QB

1
Clean the mushrooms with a damp cloth or, ideally, a small brush. In any case, never wash them with water as they will absorb it and lose all their flavour. Chop the mushrooms roughly (chopping the smallest ones in half) then brown them in a saucepan with olive oil and butter for 3–4 minutes.

2
Add the thyme, garlic, salt and pepper and continue to brown for a further 2 minutes. And you're ready to go!

These mushrooms are delicious with braised meat or some polenta. Ideal comfort food for lazy Sundays or rainy days – all the better if shared with the family.

A MINUTE TO SPARE?

Now's the time to hang out the clothes you put in the washing machine hours ago. Can you remember the song that was in your head earlier?

PiZZe

FOCACCIA ALLA STRACCIATELLA

Focaccia with stracciatella and heirloom tomatoes

<u>PER 4 AMICI</u>
(you won't feel like sharing it with any more people, anyway)

- 1 cooked focaccia *(or turn to page 304 to learn how to make your own, if you fancy that)*
- 5 heirloom tomatoes
- 100g (3½oz) Parmigiano Reggiano, in shavings
- 250g (9oz) stracciatella
  200g (generous ¾ cup) *pesto alla genovese (if you want to make your own, find out how on page 284)*

- 1 bunch basil
- Fresh oregano QB
- Salt QB
- Pepper QB
- Extra-virgin olive oil QB

1
Chop the tomatoes into slices around 1cm thick then marinate them in a salad bowl with oregano, basil leaves, a few pinches of salt, some freshly ground pepper and a good drizzle of olive oil (or even 2 splashes – don't hold back).

2
Split the focaccia down the sides. You now have a top and a bottom, as in a burger bun. Arrange the tomatoes on the bottom, along with some fresh basil leaves and a generous helping of pieces of stracciatella.

3
Add a few spoonfuls of the wonderful pesto you now know how to make. Drizzle on some olive oil (yes, even more olive oil – Italians drink it for breakfast, so we can never have too much of it), and season with a pinch of salt and a little more pepper. Finally, sprinkle on the shavings of Parmigiano and close the focaccia.

In Italy, a range of small sandwiches are set down in the middle of the table so that everybody can help themselves, with a glass of spritz or wine to wash it down – *magnifico!*

A MINUTE TO SPARE?

Check how many wine glasses you have in the cupboard, it would be awkward to run out when guests arrive. There's always time to ask your neighbour.

FOCACCIA DI FOLLIA

Focaccia with mortadella and *pesto alla genovese*

PER 4 AMICI
(you can share, but only if you feel like it)

- 1 cooked focaccia *(or, if you prefer, learn how to make your own on page 304)*
- 600g (1lb 5¼oz) mortadella

- 200g (generous ¾ cup) *pesto alla genovese (we explain how to make your own on page 284, if you have enough time)*

1   Split the focaccia down the sides. You now have a top and a bottom, as in a burger bun. Liberally spread pesto over the insides of the focaccia. Then add slices of mortadella and tuck in!

2   For serious connoisseurs: stuff in some stracciatella. Italians often enjoy this focaccia under a beach parasol, but it tastes just as good on a grey wintry day in November. It's the gift that keeps on giving, all year round.

A MINUTE TO SPARE?

Start thinking about topics of conversation that would go down well over the dinner table. Anything to avoid an uncomfortable silence…

FOCACCIA ALLA PARMIGIANA

Focaccia with aubergines, Datterini tomatoes and mozzarella

PER 4 AMICI

- 1 cooked focaccia *(or turn to page 304 to learn how to make your own, if you fancy that)*
- 2 aubergines
- 150g (5½oz) Datterini tomatoes
- 2 buffalo mozzarellas (125g/4½oz each)
- 50g (⅓ cup) plain flour
- 1 bunch basil
- Sunflower oil QB
- Extra-virgin olive oil QB
- Salt QB
- Pepper QB

---

1 Chop the aubergines into slices about 1cm wide. Dip them into the flour then transfer them to a heavy-bottomed saucepan with hot sunflower oil (170°C/340°F) and deep-fry them. Once they are cooked, transfer them to a sheet of kitchen paper to absorb any excess oil.

2 Chop the tomatoes in half and put them in a bowl with a drizzle of olive oil, a few basil leaves, and some salt and pepper. Mix thoroughly.

3 Split the focaccia lengthways. You now have a top and a bottom, as in a burger bun. Put tomatoes, aubergine slices and generous pieces of torn mozzarella inside the focaccia, along with a little salt and pepper and some extra basil leaves – *e basta*. Close it up and take a big bite. *Goditela!*

A MINUTE TO SPARE?

Don't think twice about lighting some candles, putting on some music and creating a cosy atmosphere. Even if it's only for a focaccia.

FOCACCIA DI HAMICI

Focaccia with cooked ham and Comté cheese

PER 4 AMICI

- 1 cooked focaccia *(or turn to page 304 to learn how to make your own, if you fancy that)*
- 300g (11oz) Comté
- 600g (1lb 5¼oz) ham cooked with herbs
- 1 tbsp wholegrain mustard *(because you're a bougie chef)*
- 1 egg

- 1 tsp white wine vinegar
- 150ml (⅔ cup) sunflower oil
- Salt QB
- Pepper QB

1
To make the mayonnaise, use a hand mixer to blend the egg, sunflower oil, white wine vinegar, salt and pepper. A tall measuring jug works well for this (that vase will do – we all prefer mayo to flowers, anyway). Once the sauce is thick and smooth, put aside at room temperature. It will need at least 5 minutes to stabilize. Then, mix in the tablespoon of mustard.

2
Split the focaccia down the sides. You now have a top and a bottom, as in a burger bun. Put the Comté in the centre, in thick or thin slices (as you wish, it's your sandwich), add the ham and spread the mayonnaise on the top slice of the sandwich (preferably on the inside, otherwise your hands will end up very messy indeed). Put the 2 halves of the focaccia together. *A tavola!*

A MINUTE TO SPARE?

Have you shaved? Have you waxed your legs? We reckon you've still got time.

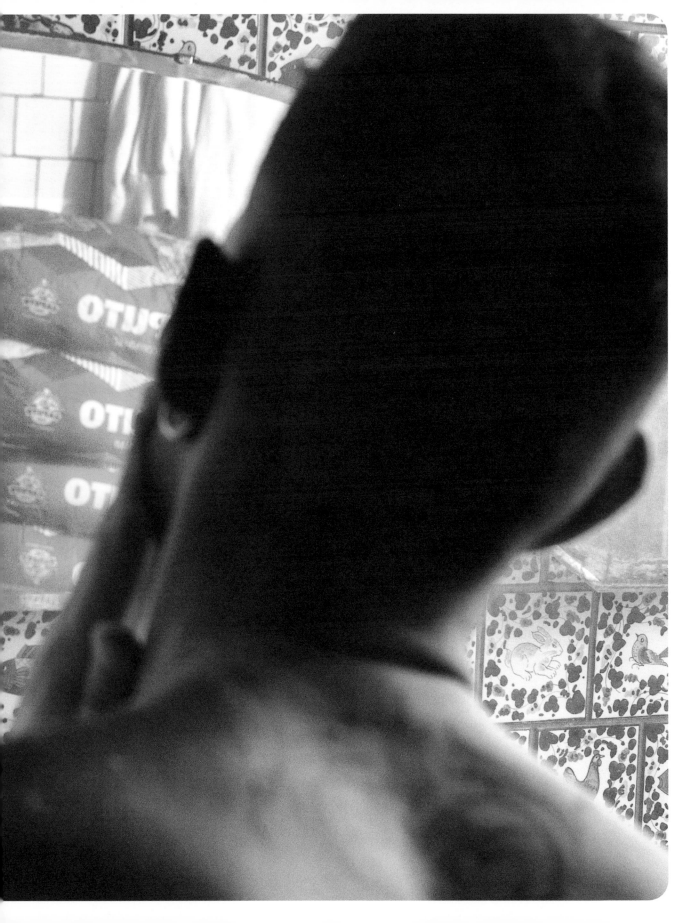

PIZZA ROSSA MANIA

Red pizza with pesto, stracciatella and olives

PER 4 AMICI

For the pizza dough
- There's a recipe for homemade dough on page 302, but if you leave work exhausted after a long day, feel free to buy your ready-made pizza dough in a deli or bakery.
- 1 tin peeled tomatoes
- 150g (5½oz) stracciatella

- 70g (scant ½ cup) Taggiasche olives
- 100g (scant ½ cup) *pesto alla genovese (we explain how to make your own on page 284, if you have enough time)*
- Extra-virgin olive oil QB
- Basil QB

1 Roll the dough out on an oven tray. Spread peeled tomatoes all over its surface, crushing them roughly with your hands. Add a generous drizzle of olive oil and cook the pizza in the oven at 230°C fan/250°C/480°F/GM 9 (if your oven doesn't go that high, take it as far as you can — just get it hot in there) for around 15 minutes, or until it has taken on a nice golden colour.

2 Cover the pizza in loadsa stracciatella and basil leaves. Then add a few spoonfuls of pesto and some olives, and we're off!

Serve in the centre of the table, slice and enjoy with your hands surrounded by loved ones.

A MINUTE TO SPARE?
Check whether there is any ice in the freezer. If not, save your aperitif by asking your guests to bring a bag of ice. PHEW!

PIZZA COPPACABANA

Pizza with burrata and slices of coppa

PER 4 AMICI

For the pizza dough
- There's a recipe for homemade dough on page 302, but if you're short of time and your friends are about to show up, you have our permission to buy dough in a deli or bakery.
- 3 burratine (125g/4½oz each)

- 300g (11oz) coppa
- 1 bunch basil
- Extra-virgin olive oil QB
- Fior di sale QB
- Pepper QB

1 Roll the dough out evenly on an oven tray, drizzle on plenty of olive oil and a few pinches of fior di sale. If you want something a little tastier, you can add some oregano leaves or Espelette pepper (or both, if that's what you fancy). Cook the pizza in an oven at 230°C fan/250°C/480°F/GM 9 for around 15 minutes and then leave it to rest for at least 10 minutes.

2 Then, tear your burratine into large pieces and scatter them all over the surface. Finally, add the slices of coppa and the basil leaves. Grind on some pepper to set it all off and there you go – your own *dolce vita*!

In Alberto's family, on pizza nights the cooked dough was put in the middle of the table so everyone can add their own toppings to their slice. An Italo sundae party!

A MINUTE TO SPARE?

Uncork a good bottle of wine, because that plonk your best friend always brings will taste better when you're onto your second bottle.

PIZZA MOZZABELLA

Pizza with Prosciutto di Parma, tomatoes and mozzarella

PER 4 AMICI

For the pizza dough
- You'll find the recipe for homemade pizza dough on page 302, but if you have just heard the doorbell, then it's fine to fall back on some ready-made dough from the deli or bakery.
- 300g (11oz) Prosciutto di Parma
- 200g (7oz) Datterini tomatoes, sliced in half

- 3 buffalo mozzarellas (125g/4½oz each)
- 2 sprigs of thyme
- Fresh oregano QB
- Basil QB
- Extra-virgin olive oil QB
- Fior di sale QB
- Pepper QB

1   Roll the dough out evenly on an oven tray. Drizzle on plenty of olive oil, add a few pinches of fior di sale and then place the tomatoes on top, with their round side facing down. Sprinkle on salt, thyme and lots of love.

2   Put the pizza in the oven at 230°C fan/250°C/480°F/ GM 9 (if your oven goes that high – the point is to make it really, really hot in there) for around 15 minutes, or until it takes on a nice golden colour. Then leave the pizza to cool for about 10 minutes.

3   Tear off big chunks of mozzarella and scatter them over the surface of the pizza. Add some slices of Prosciutto di Parma, basil leaves, fresh oregano and freshly ground pepper.

Piano piano, you still have to wait a few minutes. However enticing the pizza may look, it's still far too hot and you have to wait for the mozzarella to melt and the fat on the Prosciutto di Parma to turn clear. YUM!

A MINUTE TO SPARE?

Good news comes when you least expect it, so pop a bottle of champagne in the fridge, as it's never as fun at room temperature. Even if you're alone tonight, everyone deserves a glass of fizz.

PIZZA PRIMAVERA

White pizza with spring vegetables and mozzarella

PER 4 AMICI

For the pizza dough
- There's a recipe for homemade dough on page 302, but if you don't feel up to it tonight, we fully understand if you buy some ready-made dough in a deli or bakery.
- 1 aubergine
- 1 courgette

- 1 yellow pepper
- 200g (7oz) mozzarella
- 1 bunch basil
- Extra-virgin olive oil QB
- Salt QB
- Pepper QB

1 Slice the vegetables finely (as thin as you fancy) and lay them on a baking tray, drizzle on some olive oil and season with salt and freshly ground pepper. Put under the grill for around 7–8 minutes. Our chef Albi puts aside a few slices as a raw garnish, but you're the boss tonight so it's up to you.

2 Roll the dough out evenly on another oven tray, Drizzle on some olive oil and add some thinly sliced pieces of mozzarella.

3 When the vegetables are almost browned, arrange them on the pizza dough, along with the rest of the mozzarella. Put the pizza in an oven at 230°C fan/250°C/480°F/GM 9 for 15 minutes, or until it takes on a lovely golden colour. Leave the pizza to rest for about 10 minutes then add some basil leaves (and the reserved raw vegetable slices, if you're following Alberto's tip). Superb – you're now a true *pizzaiolo*.

A MINUTE TO SPARE?

We strongly recommend that you listen to the English-language podcast 'Cinema Italiano', which throws the spotlight on Italian films, past and present, that have had limited international distribution. It's a gem.

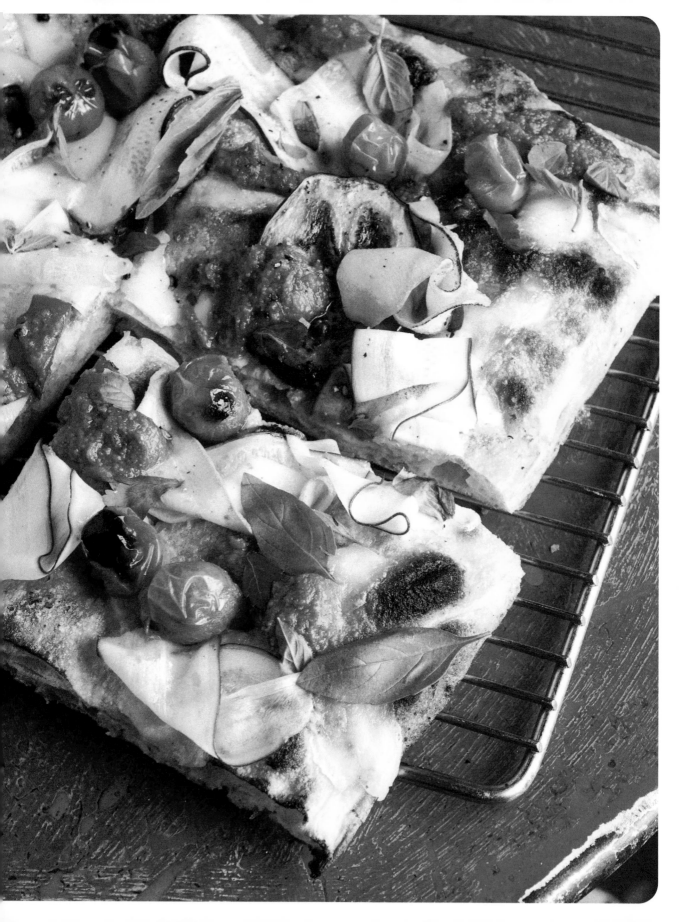

TOP 10
ITALIAN SONGS TO ROUND OFF THE EVENING

1 **'CARUSO' – LUCIO DALLA**

'Te voglio bene assaje' (meaning 'I love you no end' in Neapolitan dialect).

2 **'UNA LACRIMA SUL VISO' – BOBBY SOLO**

A perfect accompaniment to slow dancing and romance.

3 **'AMORE CHE VIENI, AMORE CHE VAI' – FABRIZIO DE ANDRÉ**

This singer was also a poet in his own right, as evident from this seductive love song.

4 **'SOTTO LE STELLE DEL JAZZ' – PAOLO CONTE**

The smooth voice of Maestro Paolo will carry you away under a starry sky.

5 **'GUARDA CHE LUNA' – FRED BUSCAGLIONE**

An ode to the moon and the sea – not to mention love: 3 ingredients guaranteed to add spice to any meal.

6 **'IO CHE AMO SOLO TE' – SERGIO ENDRIGO**

The ideal soundtrack for a carefully rehearsed marriage proposal. The title proclaims 'I love only you', so play it if that's really the case.

7 'SAPORE DI SALE' – GINO PAOLI

Or 'The taste of salt'. If the guests themselves seem a little salty, now is the time to improvise a little joke.

8 'UNICA' – ANTONELLO VENDITTI

Just in case your guests are still unsure on what you think of them.

9 'LA CURA' – FRANCO BATTIATO

'Because you are a special person and I want to take care of you.'

10 'CON IL NASTRO ROSA' – LUCIO BATTISTI

This song just works that's all we can say.

PIZZA HAKUNA PATATA

Pizza with mushrooms, potatoes and scamorza

PER 4 AMICI

For the pizza dough
- There's a recipe for homemade dough on page 302, but if your sister-in-law turns up earlier than expected, you can always use ready-made dough from a deli or bakery. No stress.

- 200g (7oz) oyster mushrooms
- 4 big button mushrooms
- 3 potatoes
- 200g (7oz) scamorza, sliced
- Extra-virgin olive oil QB

1
Roughly chop your potatoes (it doesn't matter if the pieces are irregular, as you're going to squash them) and put them on a baking tray. Drizzle on some olive oil and roast them for 20 minutes at 180°C fan/200°C/400°F/GM 6. Meanwhile, clean and chop the oyster mushrooms. Once the potatoes have been cooking for 10 minutes, add the oyster mushrooms to the baking tray.

2
Roll the dough out evenly on another baking tray. Drizzle on some olive oil and spread on the cooked potatoes (this is where you can squash them) and oyster mushrooms, along with the slices of scamorza.

3
Put the pizza in the oven at 230°C fan/250°C/480°F/GM 9 (if the thermostat doesn't go that high, then just put it at the maximum temperature) for 15 minutes until it takes on a nice golden colour. Once the pizza is cooked, finely slice the button mushrooms over the top with a mandolin. DELISH.

A MINUTE TO SPARE?

Brush up on the names of the guests who are coming for dinner. You don't want to start the night by forgetting Paul from work's name...

PIZZA RACHEL GREEN

Pizza with courgette, provolone and mozzarella

(or 1, if you're alone)

For the pizza dough
- There's a recipe for homemade dough on page 302, but if you ever leave work with no time to spare, then you have our full permission to buy ready-made dough in a deli or bakery.
- 4 courgettes, thinly sliced
- 1 shallot

- 200g (7oz) provolone (if not, Comté will do)
- 200g (7oz) mozzarella fior di latte
- 1 bunch basil
- Sunflower oil QB
- Extra-virgin olive oil QB
- Salt QB
- Pepper QB

1
Spread out the dough on a baking tray to obtain a disc around 30cm (12in) in diameter (if you don't have a round tray, use one that is 32cm/13in wide). Leave to rest.

2
Meanwhile, brown half the courgette slices and the shallot in a saucepan with olive oil, along with salt and pepper and half a glass of water.

3
Once the courgettes are nicely golden, add a few basil leaves then blend everything to obtain a smooth paste. Leave to cool, and once the paste is lukewarm, spread it over the dough. Add slices of mozzarella and provolone then put

the pizza into the oven at 230°C fan/250°C/480°F/GM 9 (or the maximum that your thermostat can manage) for 15 minutes, or until it takes on a lovely golden colour.

4
Deep-fry the remaining courgette slices in a heavy-bottomed saucepan with piping-hot sunflower oil (around 170°C/340°F). Once the pizza is cooked, add the crispy fried courgettes, a few basil leaves and a good drizzle of olive oil – and it's ready! At our *casa* we fold slices of pizza in 2 with our hands – give it a go. In any case, keep cutlery off the table – everything tastes better when eaten with fingers.

A MINUTE TO SPARE?

Don't forget to put napkins or serviettes on the table before tucking in, as eating pizza can be a messy business – so, be prepared.

DON'T BUY SPICY OIL EVER AGAIN,

as we're going to make it together…

To make a really good spicy oil, you will need:

- 1 litre (1qt) extra-virgin olive oil
- 150g (5½oz) fresh chillies (NB: real ones that make you cry, preferably from Calabria)
- 150g (5½oz) dried chillies (also from Calabria!)

---

1 Chop the fresh and dried chillies into even slices and put them into a jar.

2 Heat the olive oil in a saucepan but make sure it doesn't smoke or burn.

3 Once the oil is hot, pour it over the chillies. Close the jar and leave it to rest for at least 2 weeks. The longer it rests, the spicier it becomes.

4 You could wait for months or even years, if you think you can stand the heat. It will be, without question, the best vintage in your kitchen.

PIZZA LOOKING FOR TRUFFLE

Pizza cacio e pepe with black truffle

PER 4 AMICI

For the pizza dough
- There's a recipe for homemade dough on page 302, but if you're feeling uninspired today, then you can always buy some ready-made dough in a deli or bakery. That will work just fine!
- 250g (9oz) Pecorino Romano, grated

- 150g (5½oz) mozzarella fior di latte
- 1 black truffle, grated
- Fior di sale QB
- Extra-virgin olive oil QB
- Black pepper QB

1
Roll the dough out evenly on an oven tray, drizzle on plenty of olive oil and sprinkle on a few pinches of fior di sale.

2
Put the grated Pecorino Romano in a salad bowl and grind black pepper (generously) over it. Add half a glass of warm/hot water from the tap (around 55°C/130°F). Set aside.

3
Cover the pizza dough with large chunks of mozzarella and put it into an oven heated to 230°C fan/250°C/480°F/GM 9 for around 15 minutes.

4
Once the pizza has taken on a nice golden colour, remove it from the oven and pour over the whisked cheese mixture and grated black truffle. We suggest that you wait until everybody's sitting round the table before doing this final step, so you can show off. Anybody who doesn't clap, doesn't get pizza.

A MINUTE TO SPARE?
Look through the pages of this book and find (then plan?) your recipe for tomorrow night. A feast a day, is a must.

PIZZA O CARBO MIO

Pizza carbonara with guanciale and pecorino

PER 4 AMICI

For the pizza dough
- There's a recipe for homemade dough on page 302, but if you don't fancy flour all over the place, then you can always pop into a deli or bakery to buy some ready-made dough.
- 150g (5½oz) guanciale

- 250g (9oz) Pecorino Romano, grated
- 150g (5½oz) mozzarella fior di latte
- 4 egg yolks
- Extra-virgin olive oil QB
- Fior di sale QB
- Black pepper QB

1
Roll the dough out evenly onto an oven tray, drizzle on plenty of olive oil, add several pieces of mozzarella, a little bit of *amore*, and sprinkle on a few pinches of fior di sale.

2
Put in an oven at 230°C fan/250°C/480°F/GM 9 (or at its maximum temperature if it doesn't go that high) for around 15 minutes or until the pizza is nicely golden. Meanwhile, chop the guanciale into small matchsticks, brown them in a frying pan then set aside.

3
Put the egg yolks into a bowl, along with the pecorino, half a ladleful of warm/hot water (around 55°C/130°F) and plenty of ground pepper (remember that '*carbonara*' means 'coal' in Italian) and whisk vigorously.

4
Add the guanciale and then drizzle the egg mixture over the cooked pizza. Delicately does it, she's a special pizza, so no rushing. TO THE MOON!

A MiNUTE TO SPARE?

Check you have everything you need before you start the movie or TV show. Nobody wants to get up for salt or more wine once it's started.

A DEEP-DIVE ON ITALIAN PIZZAS

1 ROMAN PIZZA

For fans of a super-thin, crusty pizza. How can you achieve this?
With a baking temperature of 250–270°C (480–520°F) (lower than that of the
Neapolitan version) and with less water in the dough, so you get an even texture.
It's sublime – it has to be tasted to be believed.

2 NEAPOLITAN PIZZA

This is the most famous pizza of all. Distinguished by its puffy edges (we like to call
this the *cornicione* – after the cornicing on old buildings) and a thinner dough in
the middle. It is cooked at 400–500°C (750–930°F) very quickly. During this short
time, hot air is pushed out to the edges of the dough. This explains why they are so
beautifully soft and pillowy. Golden rule: eat your crusts!

3 PIZZA AL TAGLIO

Pizza by the slice, as found in food markets. This dough is very light and
cooked at a low temperature (200–300°C/390–570°F). This is cool for a pizza(!),
and it also makes it easier to reheat. Another perk, ordering by the slice means
you get to try allll the pizzas.

PIZZA CAPRESE

Super-fresh caprese pizza with tomatoes, mozzarella and basil

PER 4 AMICI

For the pizza dough
- There's a recipe for homemade dough on page 302, but if your guests have turned up with tummies rumbling, you can always resort to ready-made dough from a deli or bakery
- 100g (3½oz) Parmigiano Reggiano, grated
- 3 buffalo mozzarellas (125g/4½oz each)
- 4 large heirloom tomatoes (*Green Zebra, Black Crimean, Beef, Pineapple...the full rainbow!*)

- 100g (3½oz) Datterini tomatoes
- 1 bunch of fresh basil
- Extra-virgin olive oil QB
- Fior di sale QB
- Pepper QB

1   Roll the dough out evenly on an oven tray. Drizzle on plenty of olive oil, sprinkle on some Parmigiano and a few pinches of fior di sale, and grind on a little pepper. Put into an oven heated to 230°C fan/250°C/480°F/GM 9 for around 15 minutes (but take it out before then if it's sufficiently browned).

2   Once the hot pizza is removed from the oven, add some alternating slices of tomato and mozzarella (we love tearing it with our hands), along with a few basil leaves and another glug of olive oil.

And enjoy, your summer holidays are not over, you're in Capri in your kitchen!

A MINUTE TO SPARE?

Decide on the film you're going to watch later. You don't want to let your pizza get cold while you're fiddling about with the remote control.

PIZZA GET FIGGY WITH IT

Pizza with figs, caciocavallo and almonds

For the pizza dough
- There's a recipe for homemade dough on page 302, but if ever you're behind schedule and have run out of eggs, you can always fall back on ready-made dough from a deli or bakery.

- 250g (9oz) figs (more or less), sliced
- 300g (11oz) caciocavallo
- 120g (4oz) mozzarella fior di latte
- 100g (⅔ cup) toasted almonds
- Fresh oregano leaves QB

1
Roll the dough out evenly on an oven tray, scatter on several pieces of mozzarella and ⅔ of the caciocavallo, then put the pizza in a hot oven heated to 230°C fan/250°C/480°F/GM 9 (or the maximum your thermostat will allow) for about 15 minutes, or until it has taken on a nice golden colour.

2
Remove the pizza from the oven and scatter over some fig slices and toasted almonds. Now for the finishing touches: finely slice the remaining caciocavallo over the top (using a mandoline) and complete with a few oregano leaves. Serve the pizza on a rustic wooden board, and soak in all the admiring looks from your guests.

A MINUTE TO SPARE?

Use the time to make your own spicy oil for future pizzas (although not this particular recipe, as the oil has to infuse for a week or 2). Turn to page 217 for the recipe.

PIZZA YAS QUEEN!

Pizza with mushrooms, ham and mozzarella

PER 4 AMICI

For the pizza dough
- There's a recipe for homemade dough on page 302, but if your in-laws have just uncorked the champagne, you have our full permission to fall back on ready-made dough from a deli or bakery (after all, you don't want your champagne to go flat).
- 200g (7oz) ham

- 300g (11oz) mozzarella fior di latte
- 150g (5½oz) mushrooms *(button and oyster mushrooms, although you can also use small ceps or porcini if you're feeling fancy)*
- Marjoram leaves QB
- Extra-virgin olive oil QB
- Parmigiano Reggiano QB

1 Roughly chop and brown ⅔ of the mushrooms in a saucepan with olive oil.

2 Roll the dough out evenly on an oven tray. Drizzle on plenty of olive oil and arrange several pieces of mozzarella and ham on top, along with the cooked mushrooms. Put into an oven heated to 230°C fan/250°C/480°F/GM 9 (or the maximum that your thermostat can manage) for around 15 minutes, or until the pizza has taken on a nice golden colour.

3 Remove from the oven and, using a mandoline, finely slice the remaining raw mushrooms on top, scatter on some marjoram leaves, and add another drizzle of olive oil.

4 As an extra treat, shave over some Parmigiano and add a few grinds of black pepper. Your father-in-law will praise your culinary skills until the end of time – so it's worth the effort!

A MINUTE TO SPARE?

Try to sneak away a slice (or 2) for tomorrow's lunch. It's going to be far more tasty than that shop-bought sandwich.

DOLCI

SAVOIARDI
Sponge fingers Italian style

PER 4 AMICI

- 4 eggs
- 75g (⅓ cup) granulated sugar
- 75g (½ cup) plain flour
- Icing sugar QB
- 1 pinch of salt

---

1 Separate the egg whites from the yolks. Put the yolks in a bowl, along with 25g (⅛ cup) granulated sugar. Whisk them to obtain a smooth, even texture.

2 In another bowl, use a hand mixer to beat the egg whites, along with the pinch of salt. You don't have a hand mixer? Ask a neighbour to lend you theirs, or, if you feel up to it, you can whisk the egg whites by hand. Either way, you're looking for stiff peaks.

3 Use a spatula to gently fold half of the flour and half of the egg whites into the sugary yolk mixture; repeat this process with the rest of the flour and egg whites.

4 Put the mixture in a piping bag (or a freezer bag with the corner cut off, watch out MacGyver!). Pipe out round sausages of dough around 10cm (4in) long. Make sure to pipe them spaced well apart, otherwise they'll merge into one nice big cake.

5 Sprinkle the icing sugar on top and put into an oven heated to 160°C fan/180°C/350°F/GM 4 for 10 minutes. Once the sponge fingers are cooked, remove them from the oven and leave to cool at room temperature. These delicious golden *savoiardi* will fill your kitchen with a lovely aroma. The smell of an Italian holiday without even leaving your home!

A MINUTE TO SPARE?

Take the opportunity to perfect your Italian. '*La mamma*' = 'mum'. '*I pantaloni*' = 'trousers'. '*Calzone*' = 'trouser leg', though it's also a type of pizza.

TIRAMISÙ AL PISTACCHIO

Our pistachio version of the classic

PER 6 AMICI
(although we advise you to invite fewer people so you can have some leftovers for the following day)

- 25 savoiardi, aka sponge fingers *(see the previous recipe if you fancy making them yourself)*
- 500g (2¼ cups) mascarpone
- 500ml (2 cups) double/whipping cream
- 4 egg whites
- 90g (scant ½ cup) granulated sugar
- 15g (2oz) icing sugar
- 180g (6½oz) pistachio paste *(available in all Italian delis: 80g (3oz) go into the cream you're going to make,* the other 100g (3½oz) into the coulis)
- 300ml (1¼ cups) Baileys
- 200ml (¾ cup) unsweetened condensed milk
- 300ml (1¼ cups) water

For the decoration
- 150g (1¼ cups) shelled whole pistachios

---

1 Arrange the pistachios on a baking tray and put them into an oven heated to 160°C fan/180°C/350°F/GM 4 for 10 minutes. The idea is to make them lovely and golden. Once they are ready, remove the baking tray and set aside.

2 Now turn to the preparation of the coulis by putting 100g (3½oz) of the pistachio paste, the icing sugar and the condensed milk into a bowl. Combine them to obtain a smooth, glossy cream. Set aside.

3 Put the Baileys into a bowl with the water (at room temperature) then pop the bowl into the fridge. Whisk the egg whites and the granulated sugar in another bowl using an electric hand mixer (or a hand whisk, if you're feeling fit). You're aiming for an even consistency.

4 Add the mascarpone and the cream then whisk some more, until the mixture is as smooth as an Olympic ski run. Add the remaining 80g (3oz) of pistachio paste and beat some more, this time using a rubber spatula.

5 Now dip your sponge fingers into the cooled bowl of Baileys, on both sides, and then arrange them side by side in a baking dish (designed for around 6 people). Pour half the cream and some of the coulis on top. Scatter over some toasted pistachios, then repeat with a new layer of both the cream and the coulis, finishing off with a lovely crust of toasted pistachios. Put this naughty treat in the fridge for at least 4 hours (all good things come to those who wait). *E buon appetito!*

A MINUTE TO SPARE?

Listen to an episode or 2 of the podcast 'Prince Street', from the distinguished team behind Dean & DeLuca. A culinary deep-dive into the love between people and food, with a few celebs thrown in for good measure.

PASTICCIOTTI PUGLIESI

Golden shortbread biscuits with vanilla-lemon cream filling and black cherries

FOR 12 PASTICCIOTTI

- 500g (1lb 1¼oz) shortcrust pastry (*we show you how to make a superb version for yourself on page 292*)
- 800ml (3⅓ cups) milk
- 200ml (¾ cup) double/whipping cream
- 10 eggs
- 150g (⅔ cup) sugar
- 80g (⅔ cup) cornflour
- 1 vanilla pod
- Zest of 2 lemons
- Wild black cherries QB
- Butter QB

1
Mix the cornflour into 100ml (⅓ cup) of the milk in a bowl (you may have to use your hands to break down any lumps). Once this paste is totally smooth, mix in 10 egg yolks and then set aside. If you don't know what to do with all those leftover egg whites, check out a cracking recipe for meringues on page 306. Go on, you deserve it.

2
Heat the remaining 700ml (3 cups) of milk in a saucepan with the cream, sugar, vanilla pod and lemon zest. As soon as the milk starts to boil, pour it over the cornflour and egg mixture, stir then pass through a sieve to obtain a lovely smooth cream. Pour this cream into a saucepan and heat gently, stirring continuously, until the cream thickens. Remove from the heat and add a knob of butter. Cover with clingfilm (in direct contact with the cream) and set aside.

3
Use a rolling pin to spread out the shortcrust pastry on a lightly floured work surface until it is 3–4mm (⅛in) thick (take care not to overwork the pastry). Cut it into rectangles of around 8 x 3 cm (3 x 1⅛in) and put them into small buttered moulds (for tartlets or macaroons – make sure the pastry pieces fit the moulds, right up to their edges) and perforate the bottoms with a fork. Fill the moulds with the cream and a few cherries, then seal them with another (slightly thinner) sheet of pastry. Make 3 small incisions on the top with a knife. Use a brush to spread the remaining egg yolk on top to give the cooked pastry a pretty glaze.

4
Put the moulds in an oven heated to 160°C fan/180°C/350°F/GM 4 for 15–20 minutes then leave to cool at room temperature. Take these little sweet treats to the table and enjoy how much nicer everyone is after having a bite.

A MINUTE TO SPARE?

Have any holiday days remaining? Start planning your next weekend in the country.

CHOCO-LOVER CRUMBLE

Crazy chocolate crumble

PER 6 AMICI

- 2 eggs
- 160g (5½oz) softened butter (*i.e., at room temperature, so you can easily knead it into the flour*) plus a knob of butter for the dish
- 120g (½ cup) sugar
- 500g (4 cups) plain flour
- 500g (2¼ cups) chocolate spread (*we strongly advise you to buy the runniest you can find*)
- 2 tsp baking powder
- Salt QB

1
Mix the flour, salt and baking powder in a large bowl. Using your fingers (grab the kids if they're around, as they'll find it fun getting their hands dirty) add, in the following order: sugar, butter and eggs. Roll your sleeves up, and get stuck in. The idea is to rub these ingredients together to form small crumbs. Leave these to rest in the fridge for about 30 minutes.

2
Take a baking dish (or any similar, fairly shallow dish that will feed 6 people) and grease the bottom thoroughly with butter to ensure that none of the crumble sticks. Spread half of the crumbs uniformly on the bottom of the dish and squash them (again with the help of kids, if possible – this is an ideal teatime recipe) to form a compact layer (you will thank us for this tip when it comes to serving). Put the dish in the fridge for around 10 minutes.

3
Next, distribute the chocolate spread generously over the top, before adding a final layer with the remaining crumbs. No need to squash anything this time – just leave them as they are.

4
Put the dish back into the fridge for a further 20 minutes, then transfer the crumble to an oven heated to 160°C fan/180°C/350°F/GM 4 for around 25–40 minutes (the timing will greatly depend on your oven). The crumble is ready once it's turned a lovely golden colour. Head for the kitchen table with a big cup of tea and any ravenous gremlins ready to lick their plates clean. We'll leave you to enjoy yourselves.

A MINUTE TO SPARE?

Check online to see if your favourite artist is performing soon. There's nothing like seeing them live is there?

CIAMBELLINE AL VINO

Shortbread biscuits with Chianti

Our only piece of advice is to invite loads of friends over to enjoy them.

FOR 30 BISCUITS

- 500g (4 cups) plain flour
- 150g (⅔ cup) muscovado sugar (although ordinary brown sugar will do just fine, too)
- 300g (1¼ cups + 2 tbsp) granulated sugar
- 135ml (½ cup) Chianti (or any other red wine you fancy)
- 25g (⅞oz) aniseed
- 10g (2 tsp) baking powder
- 125ml (½ cup) sunflower oil

---

1 Mix the flour, muscovado sugar, baking powder and aniseed in a bowl. Work the mixture with your fingers – that's half the fun. Then add the oil and wine (while helping yourself to a little glass) and continue mixing. You're looking for a smooth, even dough but don't overwork it, otherwise you won't be able to make nice shapes for the biscuits.

2 Form little sausages with the dough then close them in on themselves to create mini-doughnuts. Now dip these little rings into a bowl of granulated sugar and lovingly place them on a baking tray.

3 Bake them in an oven heated to 140°C fan/160°C/325°F/GM 3 for 20–30 minutes. They must be slightly browned – use your judgement. Leave to cool at room temperature, ideally close to an open window. Watch out for birds – they might be hungry too!

TIP

Make this recipe with the help of some kids, or friends who have very small dainty hands. This will mean you get lots of different shapes and sizes, which adds to the fun. Enjoy these dunked first in an alcoholic drink (wine, champagne or your drink of choice...) – it's a grown-up biscuit. No ID, no snacking.

A MINUTE TO SPARE?

Check what's coming up in your local cinemas. When was the last time you saw a good film on the big screen?

BEIGNET AND THE JETS

Chubby Venetian beignets

PER 6 AMICI

- 500g (2 cups) cow's milk ricotta
- 3 eggs
- 200g (generous 1⅓ cups) plain flour
- 60g (4½ tbsp) granulated sugar, plus a bowl of sugar as a dip for the cream puffs
- 5g (1 tsp) baking powder
- Zest of 1 orange
- 10ml (2 tsp) Pastis
- Sunflower oil QB

For the pastry cream
- 400ml (1⅔ cups) milk
- 40g (5 tbsp) cornflour
- 5 egg yolks
- 100ml (¾ cup) double/whipping cream
- 75g (⅓ cup) sugar
- 1 vanilla pod
- 1 knob butter
- Zest of 1 lemon

1
If you want to strictly follow the rules (you goody two-shoes), 2 hours before preparing the dish itself, drain the ricotta in a clean tea towel. The aim? To drain as much liquid out of the cheese as possible. Once you're ready to start, put the ricotta in a bowl with the eggs, sugar, orange zest and Pastis and combine them with an electric hand mixer (or a hand whisk, if you're very strong or have no other option) to obtain a smooth, even dough.

2
Meanwhile, combine the flour with the baking powder then sieve them over the dough. Continue whisking and try to remove any lumps. When this mixture is nice and smooth, transfer it to a piping bag and keep it in the fridge for at least 1 hour.

3
Mix 50ml (3½ tbsp) milk with the cornflour in another bowl (still watching out for lumps). Once this mixture is smooth and even, add the egg yolks and stir them in; set aside. Heat the remaining 350ml (1½ cups) milk in a saucepan, along with the cream, sugar, vanilla and lemon zest. As soon as it starts to boil, pour it (still hot) over the cornflour mixture and stir it in, then strain the liquid into a saucepan. Simmer over a low heat, stirring continuously, until the mixture starts to thicken. Once it is nice and thick, remove from the heat and add a knob of butter. Cover with clingfilm (keep it in direct contact with the cream). Set aside.

4
Squeeze out small balls (around 3cm/1¼in long) of the ricotta mixture with the piping bag then plunge these into a heavy-bottomed saucepan of boiling oil (around 165°C /330°F) and cook until they are nicely browned. (If you have no piping bag, you can use 2 teaspoons instead. Fill one with dough, and then use the back of the other to scrape it into the hot oil. Easy peasy!).

5
Drain on a sheet of kitchen paper to remove any excess grease. Then use a small syringe (or another piping bag) to stuff these plump fritters with the pastry cream. Finally, roll these golden balls into the bowl of sugar so they're naughtier than ever.

JACQUEMOUSSE

Chocolate mousse with fior di sale and olive oil topping

PER 6 AMICI

- 200ml (generous ¾ cup) double/whipping cream
- 750ml (3¼ cups) whole milk
- 5 egg whites
- 3 egg yolks
- 85g (4 tbsp) honey
- 180g (6½oz) dark chocolate
- 125g (4½oz) milk chocolate

- Chocolate flakes QB
- 1 tsp extra-virgin olive oil *(ideally, infused with a spicy or fruity flavour, according to taste – you will notice the difference)*
- 1 pinch of salt
- Fior di sale QB

1
  Heat the milk, cream and honey in a saucepan. Meanwhile, melt the 2 types of chocolate in a bain-marie. When they have completely melted, add the egg yolks (make sure that they are at room temperature, not cold) and whisk in. Pour the chocolate mixture into a stainless-steel bowl and then add the cream, milk and honey mixture.

2
  Whip the egg whites with a pinch of salt. Once the egg whites are stiff, add them to the other ingredients in the bowl in 2 stages (it is important not to beat the air out of the egg whites), using a spatula to gently fold in then leave to rest:
- All night, if you're sufficiently organized to prepare a meal the day before you serve it.

- For 4 hours, if you're sufficiently organized to prepare a meal a few hours before you serve it.
- For as long as you can, if you're pushed for time and have only just started to prepare the dessert when your guests arrive. In this case, be creative and drag out the *aperitivo*, serve 3 helpings of the main course and show your holiday photos. A good mousse must be allowed to rest.

3
  Just before serving, add a few drops of your wonderful infused oil, a few pinches of fior di sale and a scattering of chocolate flakes. *Grazie e basta*, you are perfect, and so is your mousse.

A MINUTE TO SPARE?

Rewatch the surprise appearance of Jennifer Lopez on the Versace catwalk at the Milan 2019 Fashion Week. A performance for the ages.

HOW TO PRONOUNCE THE NAMES OF ITALIAN PRODUCTS

As there are lots of Italian words in this book, we asked our Chef Filippo to help you pronounce them properly. It's time to become bilingual, or try to be. How do we really say 'bruschetta', 'focaccia' and 'funghi'?? Well, listen to Filippo's dulcet tones and repeat after him:

SIMPLY THE ZEST

Lemony almond cake with raspberry topping

PER 6 AMICI

- 4 eggs
- 120g (8½ tbsp) butter
- 60g (7 tbsp) potato flour or cornflour
- 180g (1¼ cups) almond flour
- 130g (scant ⅔ cup) sugar
- 8g (1¾ tsp) baking powder
- 100g (3½ oz) white chocolate, chopped (*leave the bar in the fridge overnight, or in the freezer for 10 minutes, if you didn't read through the recipe yesterday*)

- Zest of 2 lemons (*unwaxed – we care about your health*)
- Juice of ½ lemon

For the raspberry topping
- 200g (7oz) raspberries
- 10ml (2 tsp) lemon juice
- 40g (3 tbsp) sugar
- 2g (generous ½ tsp) pectin

1 Whisk your eggs and sugar in a bowl until thickened and light (ideally with an electric mixer, but a whisk plus a strong bicep will also work). Melt the butter (easy does it, not too hot; Chef Monia has advised that this cream is delicate, we don't want it to split or scramble) and slowly pour it over the eggs.

2 Add the potato flour and the baking powder, followed by the lemon zest and the almond flour. Pour in the lemon juice and mix everything together to obtain a smooth, even dough. Add the pieces of chilled white chocolate and stir them into the dough with a spatula.

3 Transfer the dough to a buttered mould 24cm (9½in) in diameter. Put it into an oven heated to 150°C fan/170°C/340°F/GM 4 for 30 minutes. (Don't forget to prick it with a metal skewer to test when its ready.) Meanwhile, make the raspberry topping. First, heat the raspberries with the lemon juice in a saucepan. Mix the sugar with the pectin and add it to the fruit once it has been reduced to a stew (at a temperature of around 40°C/104°F). Blend. Bring the fruit to the boil again (for 2 minutes), then transfer it to a bowl and cover it with clingfilm in direct contact with the topping. Make sure that you stir the fruit mixture thoroughly before spreading it over the top and sides of the cake. Serve your masterpiece on a pretty cake stand; it's perfect as a sweet-treat for breakfast or teatime, or with ice cream as a pudding. Monia Lisa, it's beautiful.

MONIA'S LITTLE TRICK
If the top of the cake starts to brown too quickly, cover it with aluminium foil and leave it to work its magic.

A MINUTE TO SPARE?
Read a passage from Saint-Exupéry's *The Little Prince* out loud. It doesn't matter which one – we adore every single page of this book.

XXL CHOCOLATE COOKIES

PER 6 AMICI

(2 or 3 biscuits per person, or 18 biscuits just for you)

- 90g (¾ cup) cocoa
- 450g (15¾oz) dark chocolate, chopped (*first, leave the bar in the fridge overnight, or in the freezer for 10 minutes if you didn't read through the recipe yesterday*)
- 450g (15¾oz) softened butter (*i.e., at room temperature, so you can easily knead it into the flour*)
- 3 egg yolks

- 600g (4⅔ cups) plain flour
- 360g (1½ cups) muscovado sugar (*unrefined brown sugar*)
- 15g (scant 1 tbsp) bicarbonate of soda
- 10g (2 tsp) fior di sale

1
Preheat the oven to 160°C fan/180°C/350°F/GM 4. Put the flour, cocoa, bicarbonate of soda and sugar in a bowl and combine them with your fingers. You want to end up with a fine crumble mixture free of any lumps.

2
Make a small crater in the middle of the bowl, add the egg yolks and softened butter. Rub these with the flour mixture, using your fingers, until you obtain a smooth, even dough. Make sure to use your fingertips only, so your hands don't warm the dough.

3
Add the chopped dark chocolate and stir it into the dough (it's totally fine if the dough isn't completely smooth, just don't let it get too warm).

4
Divide this mixture into small balls about 4cm (1½ in) in diameter (let's say a minimum of 55g/2oz, but above that, it's up to you – they're your cookies), place on a lined baking tray and sprinkle a pinch of salt on each one.

5
Transfer the balls to the oven. After 10 minutes, squash them flat, then return them to the oven for a further 5 minutes. The cookies should have a soft centre. Don't worry if they look partially uncooked when you take them out of the oven. Once they cool, you'll thank us.

A MINUTE TO SPARE?

Have a quick Google to find out your 'love language'; your friends and partner will find it veeeerry insightful. Fingers crossed yours is 'Words of Affirmation' as this book is full of them! You sexy minx.

PANNA WINTOUR

Panna cotta with verbena and citrus fruits

PER 6 AMICI

- 1 litre (1qt) double/whipping cream
- 50g (¼ cup) granulated sugar
- 10g (2 tsp) pectin

- Zest of 1 orange and 1 lemon
- A few fresh verbena leaves
- Some citrus fruits (*of your choice*)

1
Halve the citrus fruits and remove the flesh. Keep the skins intact and put them in the freezer. (Let's upcycle here: make a juice from the flesh and get your daily dose of Vitamin C).

2
Heat the cream in a saucepan with the verbena leaves and orange and lemon zest. Once the liquid is hot, discard the leaves and zest. If you have enough time, leave to rest with the leaves and zest for 30 minutes in a covered bowl to allow the flavours to infuse a little more.

3
Meanwhile, mix the sugar and the pectin in a bowl. Then add your citrus cream. NB: it mustn't be too hot. The ideal temperature is 40°C (104°F) – but how can you check that? Well, if you don't have a thermometer in your home, you can always ask the neighbour for one.

4
Combine all the ingredients with a hand mixer or whisk, removing any lumps. Bring the cream to the boil in a saucepan. As soon as you see small bubbles starting to appear, remove from the heat then gently pour the cream into the citrus skins you've been keeping in the freezer.

5
Keep in the fridge for as long as possible. Ideally… 4 hours! More realistically: for the length of your dinner – and here's hoping this evening's guests are tardy. For a final flourish, sprinkle some sugar on top and flambé with the grill or a blowtorch. Don't singe your eyebrows!

A MINUTE TO SPARE?

Don't forget to take photos of this masterpiece from every angle. Send one to your *famiglia* to make *nonna* proud, put one on your story and watch the likes roll in, and post one on the grid tagging Mary Berry (Our Queen).

TORTA DI MELE

Dairy-free apple pie from Monia's mamma

PER 6 AMICI

- 5 apples
- 600g (4⅔ cups) plain flour, sieved
- 250g (1 cup + 2 tbsp) brown sugar
- 15g (generous 3 tsp) baking powder
- 6 eggs

- 250ml (1 cup) freshly squeezed fruit juice *(orange, lemon, apple, etc.)*
- 150ml (⅔ cup) sunflower oil *(or any other seed oil)*
- Salt QB

1
Peel the apples then cut them into slices around 4mm (⅛in) thick. Set aside in a bowl of water with ice cubes. Meanwhile, mix the eggs with the brown sugar in another bowl to obtain a nice thick mixture. Gradually add the oil. The next part requires coordination: continuously mixing (you can do it – you're really strong!), gently incorporate the sieved flour (previously mixed with the baking powder) and the fruit juice, alternating between the two. Once the dough is smooth and even, sprinkle on some salt.

2
Now, drain the apple slices and dry them out on a sheet of kitchen paper before adding them to the dough (set a few slices aside for the final decoration). Use a spatula to gently mix the apple slices into the dough, taking care not to break them.

3
Then grease an ovenproof dish around 24cm (10in) in diameter (or line it with greaseproof paper, if you prefer), pour in the dough, and finish by adding the remaining apple slices in a pretty spiral. Put the dish in an oven heated to 155°C fan/175°C/345°F/GM 4 for 30–40 minutes (depending on your oven). (Don't forget to prick it with a metal skewer to test when it's ready.)

4
Leave to cool slightly. Serve with a scoop of ice cream, crème fraîche, or even custard – or... none of the above, if you want to be totally dairy-free . You're in charge!

A MINUTE TO SPARE?

Make sure all your guests have been invited, have your address and know how to get there. It would be sad to end up eating on your own (or maybe not – we'll leave you to be the judge of that).

FONDANT OF YOU

Chocolate fondant (for choco-lovers only)

PER 6 AMICI

- 200g (7oz) dark chocolate
- 100g (3½oz) butter
- 4 eggs

- 150g (⅔ cup) brown sugar
- 50g (⅓ cup) plain flour, sieved

---

1 Melt the chocolate in a bain-marie. When it starts to soften, add the butter then set the mixture aside to cool.

2 Separate the yolks from the egg whites, putting each in large bowls separately. Whisk the yolks in their bowl with half the sugar. Beat the egg whites into stiff peaks, along with the remaining sugar, in the other bowl.

3 Use a spatula to fold the egg whites (in 3 batches) into the yolks. Don't you knock out their air!

4 Then delicately add the flour and stir – softly, softly. Butter a mould around 24cm (10in) in diameter and pour the mixture into it. Put it into an oven heated to 160°C fan / 180°C / 350°F / GM 4 for 30 minutes.

TIP

Our chef Monia likes to remove the cake from the oven after just 20 minutes and serve it, almost cooked, with a little whipped cream or ice cream. It's a real treat!

A MINUTE TO SPARE?

Cancel your subscription to the gym – you know full well that you never go.

SAY 'CHEEEEESECAKE'

Chocolate cheesecake

PER 6 AMICI

- 500g (2¼ cups) Philadelphia cheese (or another cream cheese of your choice)
- 300ml (1¼ cups) double/whipping cream
- 3 whole eggs
- 70g (2½oz) butter

- 260g (9oz) dark chocolate (70% cocoa)
- 1 tsp cocoa powder
- 190g (¾ cup + 2 tbsp) sugar
- 1 pinch of salt

1
  Preheat the oven to 210°C fan/230°C/450°F/GM 8. Heat the cream and sugar in a saucepan over a very, very low heat for around 2 minutes, to allow the sugar to dissolve. Remove the saucepan from the heat and add the Philadelphia cheese and cocoa powder. Set aside.

2
  Meanwhile, melt the dark chocolate and butter in a bain-marie or microwave (we're relying on you to avoid burning them if you go for the microwave option). Then, combine this chocolate mixture in a bowl with the cream, mixing gently with a spatula to obtain a smooth, even paste. Use a whisk to incorporate the eggs one by one, and finally, add the pinch of salt.

3
  Now that the mix is absolutely smooth and creamy, pour it into a round mould about 24cm (10in) lined with greaseproof paper.

4
  Lower the heat of the oven (it's seriously hot by now) to 180°C fan/200°C/400°F/GM 6 and put the mould inside for 15–20 minutes. Once this little marvel is cooked, leave it to rest, first at room temperature then in the fridge for 3–4 hours. Obviously, you can always get stuck into this cheesecake as soon as it comes out of the oven, but the longer you allow it to cool, the easier it will be to serve – it's divine.

A MINUTE TO SPARE?
Take this opportunity to unsubscribe from all those terrible spams that appear in your inbox every Saturday morning.

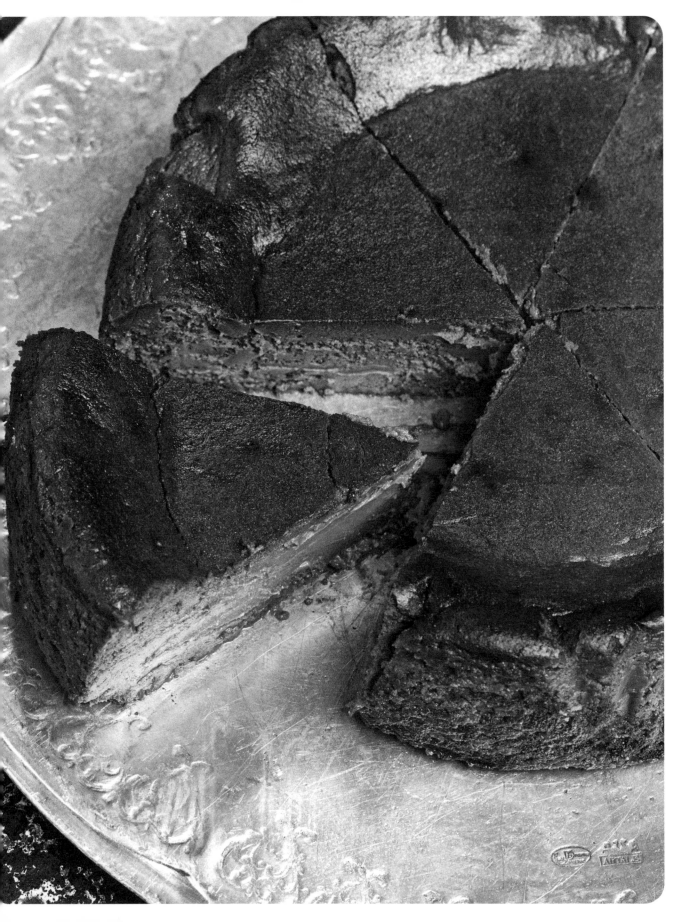

MOUSSE DI FORMAGGIO

Ricotta mousse with Amaretti biscuits
and honey-caramel coulis.

PER 6 AMICI

- 500g (2 cups) ricotta
- 350ml (1¼ cups) double/whipping cream
- 100g (3½oz) Amaretti biscuits
- 130g (1¼ cups) icing sugar
- Orange blossom water QB

For the caramel
- 300g (scant 1 cup) honey
- 50ml (3½ tbsp) maple syrup
- 200ml (¾ cup) double/whipping cream
- 150ml (⅔ cup) water
- Needles from 3 sprigs of rosemary, finely chopped

1
Heat the honey, water, maple syrup and rosemary in a saucepan. Bring the mixture to the boil and then add the 200ml (¾ cup) cream. Reduce and stir – it'll smell like heaven. Set aside till it's time to serve. See you in a while caramel!

2
Mix the ricotta, icing sugar and orange blossom water with a spatula to obtain a smooth, even paste. Then, use a whisk to whip the whipping cream into silky soft peaks.

3
Fold this cream into the ricotta mixture, again using the spatula. You want it to be light and creamy. Transfer this mixture to a piping bag (or a small freezer bag with a corner cut off).

4
Now, this is where the magic happens! Use the piping bag to squeeze the mousse into one side of a pretty bowl, arrange some small pieces of Amaretti biscuit in the centre then fill the other side of the bowl with a layer of caramel (ahhh there she is!). Add a few sprigs of rosemary on top, and serve. It'll win over the most stubborn of 'not-dessert people'.

A MINUTE TO SPARE?

For the good of the planet, send an email to your bank requesting to go paperless and no longer receive any correspondence by post.

TARTUFINI AL LIMONCELLO

Beautiful coconut balls with creamy lemon-curd

PER 6 AMICI

For the lemon curd express
- 200ml (¾ cup) lemon juice
- 10 egg yolks
- 200g (1 cup) granulated sugar

For the *tartufini*
- 200g (7oz) biscuits *(just like those Nice biscuits from your childhood)*
- 200g (scant 1 cup) mascarpone
- 300g (2½ cups) desiccated coconut
- 75g (⅓ cup) granulated sugar
- 400g (14oz) white chocolate
- 30ml (1fl oz) limoncello
- Zest of 2 limes

1
Lemon curd express
This is easy – just mix all the ingredients in a bowl.
Then you have 2 possible ways of cooking it.
- In a bain-marie: cook over a low heat while stirring continuously. The mixture should start to thicken but remain smooth and shiny. Be careful not to scramble the egg yolks.
- In a microwave: heat full blast for 10 seconds then stir. Repeat this until you obtain a smooth, even cream.
Cover the lemon curd with clingfilm and store in the fridge.

2
Tartufini
Use a mixer to grind the biscuits (eat one of them if you're feeling peckish). Combine the sugar with the mascarpone in a bowl to obtain a smooth mixture. Add the ground biscuits, limoncello and lime zest, combining the ingredients with a spatula to obtain an even texture. Cover the bowl with clingfilm and then put it in the freezer for 10 minutes. Divide the mixture into 20 pieces. One by one, spread them on the palm of one hand and use the other to add a dab of lemon curd, before closing it into a nice ball. Put these pretty *tartufini* in the freezer.

3
Melt the white chocolate in a bain-marie or a microwave. Take care not to burn it! Remove the *tartufini* from the freezer and use a toothpick to dunk each one in the melted chocolate, then in the desiccated coconut. Keep in the fridge until it's time to tuck in.

A MINUTE TO SPARE?
Treat yourself to a pedicure. You've been on your feet all day; you deserve it.

LIMONCELLO: HOW TO MAKE YOUR OWN

Limoncello comes from the south of Italy, and it owes its distinctive taste to the presence of Sorrento lemons. Traditionally, the *nonna* is responsible for making it for the whole family – and she is usually the first to sample each batch. Fishermen and farmers also drink it first thing in the morning to fight the cold. Aside from that, it has become famous as an Italian's favourite digestif. It is served in a chilled shot glass, or with ice. And it is super-important to keep your limoncello in the freezer between meals.

To make a nectar fit for the gods (around 2.5l (2²/₃qt) in quantity), you need:

• 3kg (scant 7lb) medium-size lemons *(it's hard to find Sorrento lemons outside Italy, but, whichever you buy, make sure they're high-quality and unwaxed, preferably organic, because only the zest is used here. Always pick lemons with the skin completely unblemished)*
• 1 litre (1qt) alcohol (90 proof /45% ABV)
• 1.5l (1½qt) water
• 700g (3½ cups) granulated sugar

---

1 Use a small brush to clean the lemons under cold water. Use a peeler to remove the lemons' zest. Be sure to leave behind the white pith under the skin – this would make the limoncello too bitter.

2 Put the zest in a large glass jug and fill with the alcohol. Then cover with a cloth. Leave the alcohol for at least 1 month, in a cool dark place, in order to fully infuse. Stir this mixture every day (it's worth it. Just like you!)

3 A month later, make a syrup by boiling the water with the sugar; leave to cool. Add the cooled syrup to the lemon mixture, and then filter the liquid into glass bottles. Leave to rest for a few more days before tasting. On the big day, place your bottles in the freezer and drink the limoncello chilled. *Salute!*

If you're an ambitious chef, you can use your homemade limoncello in some dishes (particularly desserts). You can make a *torta al limoncello*, a *crema al limoncello* and even a *tiramisù al limoncello*. It can also be made into an aperitivo – limoncello spritz, with 40ml (1.5oz) limoncello and 100ml (2½oz) prosecco topped up with sparkling water – *cin cin!*

PAVLOVA ANDERSON

Pavlova with red berries, coconut and lime zest

PER 6 AMICI

For the red berry coulis
- 100g (¾ cup) raspberries (frozen or fresh)
- 100g (½ cup) strawberries (frozen or fresh)
- 100g (¾ cup) blueberries (frozen or fresh)
- 80g (⅔ cup) sugar
- Juice of 1 lime

For the lime-coconut cream
- 800ml (3⅓ cups) coconut cream
- 30g (¼ cup) icing sugar
- Zest of 1 lime

For the presentation
- 6 hard meringues (we show you how to make these on page 306, but if you're short of time, shop-bought meringues will do just fine)
- 2 punnets of strawberries
- 2 punnets of raspberries
- 2 punnets of blueberries
- 120g (1⅓ cups) desiccated coconut
- Zest of 2 limes

1 First, the red berry coulis

Cook all the ingredients in a saucepan over a low heat until you obtain a smooth, even mixture. If necessary, you can always use a blender to make it even smoother – you'll want to remove any small seeds that'll get stuck between your teeth. Put the coulis in a bowl or Tupperware and leave to cool – don't worry, he's coming back later.

2 Now, make the lime-coconut cream

Whip the coconut cream, icing sugar and lime zest until the mixture is nice and fluffy.

3 Now, let's make the magic happen

In a pretty dessert bowl create a bed of coulis and some fresh red berries, then add a meringue (the idea is to create the most beautiful sandwich here). Add a generous dollop of lime-coconut cream on the base of the meringue, then a little more coulis. Spread a layer of the fresh berries on top before finally closing the pavlova with the second meringue. Finish with some lime zest and a sprinkle of dessicated coconut. Stand back and admire; your work is done.

A MINUTE TO SPARE?

Make a list of the 3 things you'd like to achieve for yourself (but also for your loved ones) in the next 6 months, and make it happen. You got this.

FIGGIN' BEAUTIFUL

Carpaccio of figs, granola, whipped mascarpone cream and raspberry coulis

PER 6 AMICI

For the granola
- 75g (⅓ cup) brown sugar
- 90g (4¼ tbsp) honey
- 50ml (scant 2½ tbsp) maple syrup
- 250g (2¾ cups) oats
- 50g (1¾oz) pecan nuts
- 75g (2⅔oz) hazelnuts
- 85g (3oz) raisins
- 100ml (scant ½ cup) sunflower oil
- Fior di sale QB

For the raspberry coulis
- 375g (13¼oz) raspberries
- 20ml (4 tsp) lemon juice
- 100g (½ cup) sugar
- 1 vanilla pod *(only if you like the taste)*

For the whipped cream
- 1 litre (1qt) double/whipping cream
- 50g (1¾oz) mascarpone
- 100g (scant 1 cup) icing sugar
- 1 vanilla pod

For the fig carpaccio
- 20 fresh figs

1

The granola

Heat the sunflower oil, honey, maple syrup, brown sugar and fior di sale in a saucepan. Remove from the heat, add the oats and mix thoroughly. Transfer the mixture to a baking tray lined with greaseproof paper and put into an oven heated to 120°C fan/140°C/275°F/GM 1 for 30 minutes. (Stir after 15 minutes.) Then, add the pecans, hazelnuts and raisins. Cook for a further 6 minutes. Cool and store this golden granola in an airtight container.

2

Raspberry coulis

Cook all the ingredients in a saucepan over a low heat until you obtain a smooth, even mixture. If necessary, you can always use a blender to make it even smoother – remove the vanilla first; you might also want to remove any small seeds that'll get stuck between your teeth. Put the coulis in a bowl or Tupperware and leave to cool.

3

The whipped cream

Whip the cream, mascarpone, vanilla seeds and icing sugar until the mixture is nice and fluffy as a cloud.

4

The fig carpaccio

Slice the figs finely, horizontally, then put 2 good dollops of the whipped cream on a pretty serving dish. Add the raspberry coulis and arrange the sliced figs on top, completely hiding the cream and the coulis. As a final touch, lovingly sprinkle some granola on top.

A MINUTE TO SPARE?

Keep some of the granola for tomorrow's breakfast, along with a spoonful of yoghurt or milk. See ya later toast!

TIRAMISSYOU
Peach tiramisu

<u>PER 6 AMICI</u>

- 150g (5½oz) Amaretti biscuits

For the compote
- 500g (1lb 1½oz) yellow peaches
- 20ml (4 tsp) lemon juice
- 50g (¼ cup) jam sugar
- 3g (½ tsp) pectin (optional)

For the peach syrup
- 100g (½ cup) peach purée
- 335g (1⅔ cups) granulated sugar

- 25ml (4½ tsp) lemon juice
- 250ml (1 cup) water
-

For the mascarpone cream
- 30ml (⅛ cups) double/whipping cream
- 500g (2¼ cups) mascarpone
- 6 egg yolks
- 90g (scant ½ cup) granulated sugar

For the decoration
- 3 peaches

1
   The compote
Wash and peel the peaches (except those you're going to use for the decoration) then dice them. Simmer 400g (14oz) of the peaches in a saucepan with the lemon juice and sugar until you get a lovely compote. If you are going to use the pectin, mix it with 15g (1 tbsp) sugar and add it to the compote. Cook for a further 2 minutes then cover the compote with clingfilm and put it in the fridge. Once it is cold, gently stir in the remaining diced peach.

2
   The syrup
Bring the peach purée to the boil in a saucepan with the sugar, lemon juice and water. Once the sugar has dissolved completely, remove the mixture from the heat. You can replace the peach purée with fresh peaches, but in this case you will have to blend them in advance. Soak the biscuits in the syrup once it is ready.

3
   The mascarpone cream
Whip all the ingredients with an electric hand mixer (or hand whisk). We want it nice and fluffy.

4
   The presentation
Remove the biscuits from the peach syrup and lay them in the bottom of a pretty baking dish. Add a layer of compote, using the bottom of a spoon to spread it on. Add ⅓ of the cream, then another layer of soaked biscuits, compote and cream. Repeat until everything has been used up.

5
   Leave to chill in the fridge for 2–3 hours. Before serving, finely slice the remaining peaches and arrange them nicely on the top of the tiramisu. This baby is going to be so good; your guests might want to skip straight to dessert.

A MINUTE TO SPARE?
Watch the incredible performance by Sister Cristina Scuccia, a Sicilian nun who won *The Voice* in Italy with flying colours.

MELA CANDITA CON CARAMELLO

Caramel candied apples on a bed of cream

PER 6 AMICI

- 6 apples
- 225g (1 cup) sugar
- 45g (1½oz) butter

- Crème fraîche QB
- 750ml (3¼ cups) cider
- 2 pinches fior di sale

---

1 Toast the sugar in a saucepan over a low heat until it turns a nice golden caramel colour. Add the butter, followed by the cider and the fior di sale.

2 Peel the apples and place them on the caramel, cook for a further 2 minutes over a medium heat then turn them over. Transfer the apples from the saucepan to an ovenproof dish and put them in an oven heated to 160°C fan/180°C/350°F/GM 4 for 30–40 minutes.

3 Turn the apples over halfway through to avoid burning the bottoms. If the contents of the saucepan are still fairly watery, you can reduce the mixture to obtain a thicker caramel.

4 Put generous dollops of crème fraîche in nice-looking dessert bowls, add an apple to each and then drizzle over the caramel – and hey presto! Giacomo's mamma would be so so so proud of you. Enjoy!

A MINUTE TO SPARE?

Plan a trip to the theatre soon. There must be a show on that you fancy in the coming weeks, and it will make a nice change to being sat on the sofa every night.

CREAM OF PASSION

Chocolate-hazelnut cream with passion fruit caramel

PER 6 AMICI

For the chocolate-hazelnut (gianduja) cream
- 665g (1½lb) gianduja
- 335ml (generous 1⅓ cups) milk

For the passion-fruit caramel
- 250g (1¼ cups) passion fruit purée
- 250g (1¼ cups) granulated sugar

- 120g (4¼oz) butter
- 100ml (scant ½ cup) double/whipping cream
- 40ml (⅛ cup) water
- ½ vanilla pod
- Salt QB

1 Bring the milk to the boil in a saucepan. Once it is hot, pour it over the gianduja and mix thoroughly. Divide this mixture between individual ramekins.

2 Use a second saucepan to bring the purée to the boil, along with the salt, cream and vanilla pod. Meanwhile, heat the sugar and water in another saucepan until you get a wonderful amber-coloured caramel.

3 Slowly add the passion fruit mixture to the caramel. Heat until it reaches the temperature of 50–60°C (120–140°F), then add the butter and leave to cool.

4 Finally, pour it over the gianduja cream in the ramekins – and revel in the taste of Piedmont.

A MINUTE TO SPARE?

Remember your New Year's resolutions. How are they going?

YOU'RE ONE IN A MILLE

Mille-feuille with caramel coulis and diplomat cream

PER 6 AMICI

For the diplomat cream and crème pâtissière (pastry cream)
- 500ml (2 cups) milk
- 3 eggs
- 10g (2 tsp) butter
- 350ml (1½ cups) double /whipping cream
- 1 vanilla pod
- 100g (½ cup) granulated sugar
- 45g (scant ⅓ cup) cornflour
- 1 sheet (around 2g) gelatine (optional)

For the caramel sauce
- 200ml (¾ cup) double/whipping cream
- 150g (¾ cup) granulated sugar
- 15g (6½ tsp) glucose powder or 15ml/1 tbsp liquid glucose
- Fior di sale QB

For the mille-feuille
- 4–5 sheets of filo pastry
- A little butter
- A little icing sugar

1
The pastry cream
Bring the milk to the boil in a saucepan, along with 50g (¼ cup) granulated sugar and the vanilla pod. Meanwhile, mix the cornflour in a bowl with the remaining 50g (¼ cup) sugar, then add the egg yolks. Pour the milk on top and mix thoroughly. Transfer this mixture to a saucepan and bring it to the boil. Add the butter and then (if using) the sheet of gelatine and stir. Leave to cool.

2
Now, on to the caramel sauce
Heat the cream and glucose in a saucepan. Set aside. Heat an empty deep saucepan. When it looks to be piping hot, pour in the granulated sugar little by little. You'll see the sugar melt and be reborn into caramel (FYI this is the Maillard reaction at work). Once the caramel turns a lovely brown colour, remove from the heat and pour over the cream and glucose mixture. Mix thoroughly, taking care not to get burnt the hot caramel. Return to the heat until you obtain a silky smooth glossy caramel. Remove from the heat a final time, add the fior di sale and mix everything together with a flourish.

3
The mille-feuille
Unfold 4–5 sheets of filo then melt a little butter in a saucepan. Brush both sides of each sheet with the melted butter, then sprinkle icing sugar over them. Lay them flat on a baking tray lined with greaseproof paper. Cook the pastry sheets in an oven heated to 160°C fan/180°C/350°F/GM 4 for 10 minutes, so that they turn crispy. Remove and leave to cool.

4
The diplomat cream
Whip the 350ml (1½ cups) of cream in a bowl then gently fold in the pastry cream with a spatula.

5
Presentation
Arrange the sheets of filo in a row, standing vertically, filling the space between them with a generous dollop of diplomat cream topped with the caramel coulis. Stand back, admire your majestic creation, then destroy it with a spoon. *Buon appetito!*

BACK TO BASICS

PESTO ALLA GENOVESE

Insane basil and pine nut pesto

Italians are crazy about pesto! It's way more than an additional extra to your meal – in fact, it's THE cornerstone of countless recipes across the Boot. Particularly in pasta and focaccias, but it's also a crazy-good accompaniment to burratas. You could almost call it 'green gold'. If your eyes turn out to be bigger than your stomach, rest assured that your pesto will keep for 4–5 days in an airtight container. Far be it for us to suggest that you're being greedy.

PER 4 AMICI

- 150g (5½oz) basil
- 60g (2oz) Parmigiano Reggiano, roughly grated
- 35g (1¼oz) pecorino, roughly grated
- 35g (¼ cup) pine nuts, toasted

- 1 garlic clove, peeled and with the middle sprout removed
- 100ml (scant ½ cup) extra-virgin olive oil
- 5g (1 tsp) coarse salt

1
Wash the basil leaves under cold water. Wipe them with a cloth to remove any moisture. If you have enough time, you can just leave them to dry for 5–10 minutes on the edge of the sink.

2
Put the garlic clove in a blender (or you can use a hand mixer). Add the toasted pine nuts. Blend until you obtain a smooth purée.

3
Now add the basil, salt and cheeses. Blend again, quickly but not at full power, to avoid cooking the basil and causing it to blacken. Drizzle in the olive oil on top and transfer the finished pesto to the fridge.

BONUS TIP

Here's how to make another version of pesto cherished by the inhabitants of Trapani, Sicily: 'pesto alla trapanese'. The cool news is that the recipe is nice and simple: just replace the pine nuts with 50g (⅓ cup) toasted almonds, blend then add 3 basil leaves and some Datterini tomatoes chopped into quarters, and blend again. A drizzle of olive on top just before serving, and BAM – a pesto with a difference!

A MINUTE TO SPARE?

Cull your clothes. We know you've been putting it off, but think how nice it'll be to be able to shut your dresser doors.

TRADITIONAL SALSA VERDE

Green sauce with anchovies, capers and eggs

Otherwise known as *'bagnet verd'* in the Piedmontese dialect. This traditional recipe is often used to accompany less noble pieces of meat (head, tongue, etc.) to make *'i bolliti'*. We prefer to serve it, however, alongside our tagliata. Epic.

PER 4 AMICI

- 20g (¾oz) anchovies preserved in oil
- 15g (2 tbsp) capers preserved in salt
- 1 garlic clove, peeled and with the sprout removed
- 2 eggs
- 100g (1 cup) breadcrumbs
- 140g (5oz) flat-leaf parsley

- 40ml (2½ tbsp) white wine vinegar
- 150ml (⅔ cup) extra-virgin olive oil
- Salt QB

---

1 Boil 2 eggs in a saucepan for 8 minutes. Reserve at room temperature. Put the breadcrumbs in a bowl and leave them to soak in the white wine vinegar for 10 minutes. Meanwhile, chop, separately, the garlic clove, parsley, anchovies and capers.

2 Once the eggs are cooked, shell them and separate the whites from the yolks. Put the yolks in another bowl and mash them with a fork to obtain a smooth paste.

3 Add the capers, garlic, vinegary breadcrumbs, parsley and anchovies. Mix thoroughly until the sauce is smooth and even. Now, stir in the olive oil.

4 Add salt *'a sentimento'*, as Virginia likes to say (that means as much as feels right to you, the chef). Watch out for your blood pressure, though, because the capers and anchovies are already swimming in salt. Finally, put the sauce on the table with several spoons, so that everybody can help themselves.

A MINUTE TO SPARE?

You can phone up your grandparents to say hello. Family is everything, after all.

FONDUE FOR 2
Parmigiano fondue (or gorgonzola if you prefer)

You can find this heavenly cream in several recipes throughout this book (Gnocchi ai 4 Formaggi on page 108, for example). It's a little miracle and we hope you'll be fond-ue of it too.

PER 4 AMICI

- 500ml (2 cups) double/whipping cream
- 130g (4½oz) Parmigiano Reggiano (or gorgonzola)

- 10g (2 tsp) coarse salt (*never fine salt – never, never*)

1
Heat the cream in a saucepan, simmering gently to reduce it. Allow the moisture to evaporate and the cream will thicken to half its size. Remove the saucepan from the heat and add the Parmigiano (or some chunks of gorgonzola).

2
Whip the mixture into a smooth cream. Pass it through a sieve (or colander) into a bowl.

3
Cover with clingfilm in direct contact with the cream. NB: this contact is essential – any space between the clingfilm and the cream would create condensation, making the sauce watery. Leave to cool for around 15 minutes to allow everything to stabilize.

A MINUTE TO SPARE?
Watch a replay of the penalty shoot-out between Italy and England in the 2020 Euros – although, if you prefer to revel in the rare event of an English victory over Italy, you could rewatch their match in the 2024 Euro qualifiers.

PASTA FRESCA

Our secret recipe for perfect fresh pasta

Italians always have some dough in the fridge, ready to make a last-minute pasta dish that'll save the day.

PER 4 AMICI

- 400g (2 ⅔ cups) 00 flour
- 4 large eggs *(or 7 small ones)*

---

1 Heap the flour on a work surface and form a crater in the top. Break the eggs into the middle of the crater then beat them with a fork, gradually incorporating more and more flour to obtain a ball of smooth dough.

2 Knead the ball for 10 minutes to make the dough really smooth (now's the time to get stuck in – make the most of it!). Cover with clingfilm and put in the fridge for at least 30 minutes. Ideally, you've had the opportunity to prepare your dough the day before. In this case, wrap the dough ball in clingfilm and put it into an airtight container, to prevent it from drying out.

A MINUTE TO SPARE?

We're going to let you in on our favourite food and wine pairing. *Spaghetti alle vongole* with the white wine *Vermentino di Sardegna*: with its intense but fresh notes, it evokes the sea. The ultimate combo to while away an evening. So, now you know what to ask for the next time you go to a wine shop.

PASTA FROLLA ITALIANA

Sweet shortcrust pastry for wonderful pies and tarts

This dough can be used not only for pies and tarts, but also for biscuits. Sweet treats are made of these!

PER 6 AMICI

- 1kg (8 cups) plain flour
- 250g (1¼ cup) granulated sugar
- 600g (1lb 5¼oz) butter, cut into cubes

- 1 egg
- 4 egg yolks
- Salt QB

1 Use a food processor to blend the flour, sugar, salt and butter. Once the dough acquires a sandy consistency, add the whole egg and egg yolks and blend again.

2 Remove the dough, knead it into a ball and cover it with clingfilm. Put in the fridge for at least 2 hours. Turn back to the list of *dolci* and may the party start.

A MINUTE TO SPARE?
Think of your 3 favourite memories in the past 2 months, to remind yourself that '*la vita è bella*'.

GLOSSARY
OF ITALIAN CULINARY TERMS

1 MANTECARE A word that has no exact English translation. It's a technique that makes it possible to extract the starch from pasta and rice by creating an emulsion between the lean and fatty parts of a dish. More specifically, it involves mixing pasta and butter off the heat to give a sauce a super creamy texture.

2 GRATTUGIARE Again, there's no exact equivalent, but it means to grate an ingredient very, very finely. Italians apply the term liberally, but especially to Parmigiano grated to a fine dust and to lemon zest.

3 AL DENTE This is THE moment, *il momento*, when pasta should be removed from water. When it is just cooked, but not too much. The literal translation is firm 'to the tooth'.

4 SCOTTA Pasta that is *scotta* has been overcooked. Not only that – it's far more difficult to digest. Set your timer – pasta is no joke.

5 ALVEOLATA When a pizza is airy or fluffy. It's the highest possible praise for a Neapolitan pizza.

MANGIA MANGIA MILANO MANGIA MANGIA MILANO

6 FORMAGGIO Beware of the trap here; it is not 'fromage' as in France. The 'r' is after the 'o' and not before. But either way, just take a bite and enjoy it. Life is short.

7 ROSOLARE This means to brown meat by cooking it very slowly. A nice word for a nice moment.

8 SCHISCETTA The lunchbox that you take to the office for your break, containing food that you prepared the day before. We hope that this book will provide you with tomorrow's *schiscetta*.

9 STRABUONO You won't even find this word in a dictionary as it's a slang term that combines *stra* (extra) with *buono* (good). We use it when a dish is particularly heavenly.

10 SBRODOLARE This is what happens to messy eaters who don't manage to get all their meal to stay in their mouth, at the expense of their clothing. The next time you splatter spaghetti sauce over your shirt, you can say you've *sbrodolato* (for a man) or *sbrodolata* (for a woman).

RAGÙ BOLOGNESE
The classic ragù using 3 meats and tomato

But let us warn you – it will take far longer than 30 minutes. Maybe even 8 times as long... The trick is to prepare the ragù in bulk and keep plenty in the freezer for a rainy Sunday when you need cheering up, or for any other time when you need 'self-care' – this is the least that you deserve.

PER 4 AMICI

- 200g (7oz) minced beef
- 100g (3½oz) minced veal
- 100g (3½oz) pork sausage meat
- 50g (1¾oz) carrots, finely chopped
- 60g (2oz) yellow onions, finely chopped
- 60g (2oz) sticks of celery, finely chopped
- 50g (3½ tbsp) tomato paste
- 250g (9oz) tomatoes, peeled *(San Marzano, ideally)*

- 1 large glass of red wine *(you drink the first half and pour the second in the pan)*
- ½ glass of whole milk
- 1 bouquet garni of your choice *(providing there's no parsley, basil or rosemary – these are taboo in this recipe)*
- Extra-virgin olive oil QB
- Salt QB
- Pepper QB

---

1 Pour olive oil into a saucepan then apply the strict 30-minute rule of Salvatore's grandmother, who is from Emilia-Romagna, the birthplace of bolognese: cook the meat very slowly for 30 minutes till it is golden brown.

2 After those 30 minutes, pour in the red wine (what's left of it) then add the chopped vegetables. A further 30 minutes later, add the tomato paste.

3 After 30 more minutes, add the peeled tomatoes, milk, bouquet garni, salt and pepper. Leave everything to simmer for 4 hours (it has to *pippiare*, or chirp, as they say in Naples).

Bravo! You've worked hard but you can see that it was well worth the effort. You've created an elixir that will guarantee to make everybody happy: you, us, and all the guests lucky enough to taste your ragù.

A MINUTE TO SPARE?
Check the mirror to ensure none of the tomato sauce has ended up over your T-shirt. If it has, don a tash and you'll look like an old Sicilian gentleman.

CHOOSING (OR MAKING) A GOOD TOMATO SAUCE

Selecting a tomato sauce in a deli requires a little detective work.
Here are the 3 clues provided by our chef Salva for your quest for a partner in crime:

1 Check the amount of sugar added to the sauce. If there's a lot, it means that the tomatoes are poor quality.
2 Make sure there are no preservatives. Only tomatoes and salt are needed.
3 Look for an organic certification. If the sauce that catches your eye is thus labelled, so much the better.

And, last but not least, the tomatoes must come from Italy. Try to shop in small neighbourhood delis as much as possible. If you're a real purist with some time on your hands, we'll show you the secrets of the ultimate tomato sauce that Albi's grandmother prepares every summer with fresh tomatoes from her garden. Once it's cooked, the whole family gathers round to put it into jars, with the youngest members entrusted with adding a few basil leaves before the lids are closed. Stock up, so you can enjoy it all year round. It can come in handy for any meal, especially in winter when the mere thought of a tomato warms the cockles of your heart.

FOR AROUND 2 JARS
(depending, above all, on the quality of your tomatoes)

- 2kg (4½ lb) Datterini tomatoes
- 2kg (4½ lb) San Marzano tomatoes
- 1 bunch of basil
- Salt QB

1
Wash the tomatoes under a cold tap, drain them carefully then chop them into large pieces. Nothing fancy called for here – everything goes straight into a saucepan. Put this pan over a low heat, adding a little salt, and leave to simmer for 2½ hours.

2
Blitz the sauce in a blender. You don't have one? In that case, pass the sauce through a strainer, using a spoon to break down the chunks of tomato. You don't have one of these, either? Then the time has come to ask your neighbours – and get to know them better.

3
Once you've got your strained sauce, add some basil leaves, and that's it – you've just made the best tomato sauce in the world.

4
If you're planning to keep it in your larder like Alberto's grandmother, make sure you sterilize your jars in boiling water for 45 minutes. Then fill them with the sauce (to around 2 cm/¾in from the top) and close them tight. Now they're ready to accompany you throughout the winter.

PIZZA DOUGH

Or how to become the best *pizzaiolo* in your neighbourhood

PER 4 AMICI

- 1kg (8 cups) flour *(ideally, type 55 flour with a minimum protein content of 12%)*
- 2.5g baker's yeast *(4g if your yeast is fresh and not dried)*
- 700ml (3 cups) water
- 30ml (¹/₈ cups) extra-virgin olive oil
- 25g (6 tsp) salt

1
Use a food processor to mix the flour and yeast, kneading for 8–10 minutes at speed no. 1 (this is important – precision is crucial when it comes to dough). Slowly dribble in 560ml (2¼ cups) water over the course of the kneading. Once the dough is smooth, add the salt and move to speed no. 2 (go go go!). Pour in the rest of the water gradually over the next 5 minutes or so. The secret for success here is to incorporate the water very gently, making sure that the dough has absorbed it fully before adding more. Then sprinkle the oil on the dough.

2
The dough is ready once it's nice and smooth and doesn't stick to the sides of the food processor. If you really want to become a professional *pizzaiolo*, then the ideal temperature at the end of the kneading process is between 23 and 25°C (73–77°F) – no more, no less.

3
Remove the dough from the food processor and mould it into a ball. Transfer this ball to a stainless-steel bowl, cover with clingfilm then leave to rest at room temperature for

1 hour. Then transfer the dough to the fridge for a further 18–24 hours. This is the secret of true *pizzaioli*, the careful maturing of their dough, which also makes it much easier to digest. If you don't have 24 hours to spare, double the amount of yeast and leave the dough to rest for around 2–3 hours at room temperature.

4
If you've opted for the 24-hour version (*bravo!* you're making pizza just like us), remove the dough from the fridge and leave it to rest (with the clingfilm still in place) for a further hour. When your sleeping beauty has slumbered enough, divide it into portions, of whatever weight you choose, on a work surface covered with a sprinkling of flour or coarse semolina. Cover the portions and leave them to rise till double their size in a container before you roll them out (reckon on around 3–4 hours, as good pizza dough is a story of love and patience).

NOW FOR SOME MATHS

Let's calculate the appropriate weight for your portions in grams. For a square pizza, multiply the size of the base by that of the height (in cm) and divide the result by 2. Example: for a container measuring 20 x 35cm (8 x 14in), you'll need 350g (¾lb) of dough. And for a nice circular pizza (for around 4 people), put 250–300g (9–11oz) of dough in a round container around 24cm (10in) in diameter. <u>Tip:</u> pizza dough is your friend. And like all real friends, it's got a good memory. This means it takes on the form of the container surrounding it. So, if you want a square pizza, leave your dough to rest in a square container. When you unpack it, it will preserve its initial shape. The same is true for a round version.

NO FOOD PROCESSOR? NO PROBLEM!

Knead by hand, sticking to the same stages. Begin with a stainless-steel bowl and, after adding salt, move to a wooden work surface, adding the water very gradually. Then follow the rest of the instructions. If the dough doesn't fully absorb the water, pause for 10 minutes then resume your manual kneading.

HOW TO ROLL OUT YOUR DOUGH

Sieve a little flour or fine semolina on a work surface. Place your portion of dough on top and spread it out with your fingers to obtain a circle around 30cm (12in) in diameter. Flip it over to ensure that it's evenly spread over the work surface. Push the air out of the dough with your fingers, going from the centre to the sides, until you end up with a lovely white dough with plump edges.

CRAZY-GOOD FOCACCIA

A thick, moist focaccia ...

... seeks a topping to fully commit to making a beautiful recipe.

PER 4 AMICI

For the dough
- 1kg (8 cups) flour *(ideally, type 55 flour with a minimum protein content of 12%)*
- 10g (2 tsp) baker's yeast *(or 24g / 2¾ tbsp if your yeast is fresh and not dried)*
- 10g (2 tsp) granulated sugar
- 600ml (2½ cups) water

- 600ml (2½ cups) extra-virgin olive oil
- 20g (1 tbsp) salt

For the brine
- 200ml (¾ cup) water
- 100ml (scant ½ cup) extra-virgin olive oil
- 5g (1 tsp) salt

---

1 Mix the flour, salt and sugar in a bowl then add the yeast. Incorporate the water and oil, then mix everything with a food processor on speed no. 1 for 9 minutes. If you're itching to get into second gear, hold yourself in check. The texture is right when the dough is smooth but neither sticky nor hard – otherwise the focaccia could end up rubbery. The ideal temperature for the dough at the end of the kneading is 23–25°C (73–77°F).

2 Mould the dough into a ball. Cover it for 10 minutes and leave it to work its magic. After that (and your quick beer break), make small portions of the weight of your choice then leave it to rest, covered, for 30 minutes.

NOW FOR THE MATHS

Calculate the weight of the dough, for a square container, in grams by multiplying the width by the height, then multiply this total by 0.7 (in cm). For example, for a container of 20 x 35 cm (8 x 14in), you'll need 490g (1 lb) of dough. Spread out the dough with a rolling pin to push out any air bubbles, lay it on a greased baking tray then finish off rolling it out with your expert fingers. While the dough is resting, prepare the brine by mixing all the ingredients with a whisk. When your dough expands to the ideal size (after about 2 hours), make some small holes here and there with your fingers. Then pour on some of the *salamoia* (brine) to fill up these holes, and leave to rest once again for 30 minutes to 1 hour. Put the dough into an oven heated to 220°C fan/240°C/475°F/GM 9 (with static heat) for 15 minutes. When the dough turns a nice golden colour, add a little more brine. And now the best focaccia of your life awaits you!

A MINUTE TO SPARE?

Wipe your wine glasses with a cloth soaked in white wine vinegar. How long has it been since you last noticed their original sheen? We consider white wine vinegar to be almost part of the family: it cleans, leaves no trace, it's the cheapest household product ever – and, what's more, you can use it with food. In short, we're huge fans.

NICE MERINGUES

An easy recipe for meringues so you stop throwing those egg whites down the sink

PER 4 AMICI

- 150g (¾ cup) granulated sugar
- 150g (1¼ cups) icing sugar
- 5 egg whites

- 60g (½ cup) coconut powder (or 60g / ⅔ cup flakes – you're the boss)

1
Preheat the oven to its very lowest setting. Beat the egg whites and the icing sugar in a bowl with an electric hand mixer (or a hand whisk, if you're strong and/or don't have an electric mixer). When the egg whites start to get fluffy, gradually add the granulated sugar to make them stiff and shiny (the consistency is perfect if a 'bird's beak' appears when you lift up the whisk). Transfer the meringue to a baking tray lined with greaseproof paper. Sprinkle coconut powder (or flakes) on top.

2
Cook the meringue in the oven for at least 3 hours. They will harden but they should remain white. Bear in mind that meringues are highly sensitive creatures: if you decide to make them on a rainy day, they won't come out well because they can't bear humidity. Moreover, egg whites are also averse to even the slightest flecks of grease, which can lead them to refuse to rise in protest.

3
If all the planets are aligned, however, and you have made too many, meringues will keep for a week – so you can nibble away at your leisure. (Be sure to store them in an airtight container.) Eat a bit more and waste a bit less – it's a win-win situation.

A MINUTE TO SPARE?
Read the poem 'Youth' by Samuel Ullman. It'll keep you young at heart...

Cool,
Appendix

LIST OF RECIPES

INDEX OF INGREDIENTS

SPARKLING WATER

Big balls theory 24
Fiori di zucca, farciti e fritti 46
Spritz-tease 31

SPICES

Aniseed
Ciambelline al vino 242

Chilli
Spicy oil 217

Nutmeg
A$ap gnocchi 122
Cannelloni della nonna Jaja
ricotta e spinaci 134
Power to the cauliflower 164
The great lasagna 120

Saffron
Risotto allo zafferano 110

SPINACH

Cannelloni della nonna Jaja
ricotta e spinaci 134

T

TOMATO

Beef tomato
Friselle Bündchen 32

Canned tomatoes
Polpo Picasso 154

Cherry tomatoes
Tarte Tatin di Manie 78

Datterino tomato
Big caprese 138
Caponata goals 168
Carpaccio diem! 84
Focaccia alla parmigiana 196
Friselle Bündchen 32
Melanzane a funghetto 176
Pizza mozzabella 206
Pizza caprese 224
Polpo Picasso 154
Tarte Tatin di Manie 78

Heirloom tomato
Big caprese 138
Bruschetta caprese 70
Focaccia alla stracciatella 190
Pizza caprese 224

Peeled tomatoes
Pizza rossa mania 202
Ragù bolognese 298
Spaghetti all'arrabbiata 94

Tomato paste
Ragù bolognese 298

Tomato sauce
Mozzarella turnovers 76
Orecchiette al pomodoro 130
Rigatoni alla vodka anni 80 98

Vine ripened tomatoes
Caponata goals 168
Pappa al pomodoro 54
Pomodori gratinati 64

V

VANILLA

Beignet and the Jets 244
Figgin' beautiful 272
Mela candita con
caramello 276
Pasticciotti Pugliesi 238

VEAL

Bruschetta vitello tonnato 36
Cotolette alla bolognese 146
Ragù bolognese 298
Scaloppine della mamma 150

VINEGAR

Balsamic vinegar
Tarte Tatin di Manie 78

Cider vinegar
Big veggie kebabs 158
Cipolline borettane 178

Red wine vinegar
La Dolceviche 74

White wine vinegar
Caponata goals 168
Focaccia alla parmigiana 196
Friselle Bündchen 32
Jon Bon Chovy 56
Julius Caesar 160
Leeks grigliati 60
Power to the cauliflower 164
Traditional salsa verde 286

W

WINE

Red wine
Big balls theory 24
Bunny & Clyde 140
Ciambelline al vino (Chianti)
242
Polpo Picasso 154
Ragù bolognese 298
Risotto alla monzese 106

White wine
Big balls theory 24
Risotto al funghi 102
Risotto allo zafferano 110
Scaloppine della mamma 150
Spaghetti vongole e bottarga
118
Zucchine alla scapece 170

WORCESTER SAUCE

Julius Caesar 160

GRAZIE MILLE
<3

A thousand thanks to our chefs, who made the magic happen with these Big Mamma recipes. Special mention to Alberto Suardi, Virginia Baldeschi, Monia Di Liello, Stefano Croella, Michele Monte, Fabrizio Rossi, Giacomo Maratia, Giuseppe Marrazzo, Michela Madeo, Sonia Dezio, Marco Spadavecchia, Francesco Vitale, Chloé Belliard, Jelena Stojanovic, Salvatore Taurisano, Edoardo Bernini, Giuseppe Morciano, Roberto Pagliuca, Éric Azoug and Mehdi Karamane, Mattia Maccheli, Andrea De Michele, Filippo La Gattuta and all the other great chefs behind the dishes in this book. To Scarlette Martin Casanova, Brando Zarghetta, Marion Greco, Filippo Di Giuseppe, Julia Markowitz, Leonardo Iori and Monika Banasik for their expert advice and culinary secrets.

Big up to all our suppliers and their wonderful produce, to all the great artisans (artists in their own right) behind each and every one of our dishes, who have accompanied us right from the start and have never stopped believing in us. This book is all about hearty recipes, top-class produce and showers.

We decided to immortalize in 6 Big Mamma–style snaps a bathroom moment just prior to the arrival of guests. Enormous *big up* to our top chefs who agreed to swap their white aprons for an octopus or a crate of lemons — we love you. A (very) big thank you to Thomas Fournier for welcoming us, along with our chef Monia and our 27m (89ft) of fresh pasta, to his chic Italian bathroom created from sketches by artists from the Concina architecture and interior design studio. Mégane Servadio, who didn't bat an eyelid when we showed up with the great chef Virginia and a fresh octopus in her summery bathroom designed by Servadio. Apolline and her bathroom with a view, which played host to our 48kg (106lb) of ham and our chef Filippo for a quick bath. Mathilde, who didn't think twice about giving over her bathroom-library (and all the rest of her house) to our chef Albi and his 1,001 recipes for an improvised feast. Théodore et Calypso, who opened the door to their lovely pink bathroom, the day before leaving on holiday, to immortalize Andrea and his 14 crates of lemons.

To everybody in our incredible team, who turn the Big Mamma adventure into a crazy story that continues every day. To Evie Horsell, our very own Shakespeare, Laura Maniscalco and her dedication for Italian produce (and spelling!), Charlotte Martinez and Mari Volkosh for their constant guidance and sharp eyes. To Clémentine Philippon, Peppe Cacciapuoti, Victor Lugger and Tigrane Seydoux for bringing this book to life.

Quarto

This edition first published in 2024 by White Lion Publishing
an imprint of The Quarto Group.
One Triptych Place, London, SE1 9SH
United Kingdom
T (0)20 7700 6700
www.Quarto.com

A catalogue record for this book is available from the British Library.

ISBN 978-0-7112-9256-7
EBOOK ISBN 978-0-7112-9257-4

10 9 8 7 6 5 4 3 2 1

Recipe photographs: Clémentine Passet
Bathroom photographs: Jean-Baptiste Strub
Team photographs: Valentin Cheli and Luca Nardone
Cover illustrations: Egle Zvirblyte
Interior illustrations and graphic concept: Charlotte Palm
and Mathilde Vogt from the studio created Big Mamma
Layout: Jérôme Cousin and Nicolas Galy for NoOok
Translation from French by Matthew Clarke in association with
First Edition Translations Ltd, Cambridge, UK.

10 9 8 7 6 5 4 3 2 1

Printed in China